FCE ⑤

D1492393

30131 04536009 3

GRANDDAUGHTER OF THE WINDRUSH

GRANDDAUGHTER OF THE WINDRUSH

Barbara Maria Nnaemeka

Book Guild Publishing
Sussex, England

First published in Great Britain in 2013 by
The Book Guild Ltd
Pavilion View
19 New Road
Brighton, BN1 1UF

Typesetting in Garamond by
Nat-Type, Cheshire

Printed and bound in Great Britain by
CPI Group (UK) Ltd, Croydon, CR0 4YY

A catalogue record for this book is available from
The British Library.

ISBN 978 1 84624 841 2

*To my husband, Frank; my children, Semper,
Tochi and Chika; my mother and father,
James and Phyllis Harris, and my
grandchildren*

*   *   *

Start by doing
What is necessary,
Then what is possible,
And suddenly you are
Doing the impossible.
   (Francis of Assisi)

Contents

Preface

This book is written for all nurses and midwives who came to Britain before me, with me and after me, and for trainee nurses, midwives and readers who are interested in the diversity of people in the global community.

The aim of the book is to share some of my experiences and perceptions of the climate that existed in the professions in the 1960s for 'overseas' trainees compared with the climate that exists in the twenty-first century.

Barbara Maria Nnaemeka

Barbados, Island of my Birth

My name is Barbara. My parents named me Barbara very soon after my birth. I was always amused when people referred to me as 'Barbara from Barbados' when I was growing up, because there was a lilt to the slogan and it appeared that people liked to say it. My parents never really explained why they chose the name; they just said that they thought it suited me.

I was born on the tiny, beautiful island of Barbados a few years after the end of the Second World War. Like many other countries, Barbados was struggling to overcome the fallout from the war. There was a marked decline in the sugar cane industry with closure of many of the sugar factories and subsequent unemployment of factory workers. This was catastrophic because the sugar cane industry was the main sustaining force of Barbados and the employer of many Bajans.

Times were hard and people struggled to survive. My parents were not exempt from the struggle and my father, who was an electrician, was forced to work in any capacity in order to eke out a living for my mother and their two children – my older sister and me, both aged less than five years. My mother was thrifty with managing the meagre rations that were available and the family never reached the level of starvation.

When I left school in 1966, I was as well versed in the history of the Wars of the Roses, King Henry VIII and the tales of Shakespeare as I was in the history of the Arawak and Carib Indians, the slave freedom fighter Bussa, Marcus Garvey and Haile Selassie, emperor of Ethiopia. My father often told us about the freedom fighter Marcus Garvey and Haile Selassie. The emperor was the symbol of hope for many black people outside Africa. I can vividly remember Haile Selassie's visit to Barbados early in 1966 and I can still visualise and feel the excitement of the crowd as they waved frantically to him when his motorcade travelled down a street near our home.

When I decided to travel to England I was optimistic about the plan: I felt that because I was a citizen of Barbados, a British colony, and I spoke English to GCE (General Certificate of Education) level, it would be like travelling from one parish to another in Barbados. A parish in Barbados is a primary division of the island. This division is similar to a county in England or a state in America, although the land mass is considerably smaller. Barbados was seen by many as the 'Little England' of the Caribbean and had centuries of connectedness with Britain. I foolishly entertained the notion that this connectedness would pave an easy path for me and the transition to England would be kind and gentle.

Unfortunately the positive perceptions of England that I had during my school days were crushed beyond immediate repair during my early years in England. Things were definitely not how I thought they would be. I reasoned then that the drastic change in my perception of England was rooted in the geography and history of Barbados. I spent many months trying to make sense of what Barbados was, in order to find a valid reason for my feelings of disappointment and betrayal.

Barbados is an island in the Atlantic Ocean with Bridgetown as the capital. It is located between the Caribbean Sea and the North Atlantic Ocean, north-east of Venezuela and south-east of Cuba. When I was a girl, I spent many days during holidays and at weekends with my family, bathing at the local beach, tasting the salty healing seawater and walking on the golden grains of sand. Those grains of sand were like microscopic coals of fire in the midday sun and unless we were wearing our rubber slippers, it was a game of walking like a crab skimming across the seabed. The beach was about two miles from our home and we often walked there; many beaches are within walking distance of the local main roads and it is not unusual for people to walk to their local beach. In spite of my visits to the beach over many years and countless numbers of sea baths, I was not able to acquire the skill of swimming. My father was an excellent swimmer and tried to teach me the rudiments, to no avail. Many years after leaving Barbados, I did learn to swim in the local pool – but only after several series of swimming lessons, a patient swimming instructor, innumerable episodes of sheer panic and the cost of hundreds of pounds sterling!

A coral island, Barbados is mainly flat with a surface area of 294 square miles (430 square kilometres). The highest point of the island is Mount Hillaby in the parish of St Andrew. The flatness of the island is very obvious when observed from the air. I once travelled by air from Miami in the USA to Barbados. The plane approached Barbados at night from the north and I was stunned by the appearance of the island. At first it was like a small dark flat figure floating in the sea. Then, as the plane skirted around the island on its approach to the airport, the figure grew larger and larger and the lights on the island increased in number and luminosity. I was breathless with excitement as I had never observed such a picturesque view of the island before. I then understood what the geographers meant by the description 'flat'.

Barbados is 21 miles (34 kilometres) long and 14 miles (23 kilometres) wide. It is incredible that the length of the island is shorter in distance than that of a marathon! I walked to school like many other children. My school was about two miles from my home and travelling was not difficult. Many others who attended the same school travelled many miles from outside the capital by bus and other means of transport. I felt lucky to live so close to the school, because punctuality was the rule irrespective of place of residence. Any late arrivals were rewarded with after-school detention. I had my fair share. The unfortunate side of the detention was that further punishment was meted out to the transgressors by their parents for arriving home late and for earning the detention in the first place. My parents were no exception, although the punishment was a thorough scolding and a long lecture on the virtues of punctuality. Parents firmly believed that the school and the teachers were always right; trying to show my parents that the teacher was harsh and insensitive was a lost cause. There was no other alternative than to show gratitude that the punishment was not more severe and promise to be a dedicated punctual pupil in future. The unwritten rule was to rise with the sun, get organised and leave home on time to avoid tardiness and detention. A child could perceive an island as a great big continent on the journey to school, especially when the seconds seemed to be ticking away at twice the normal speed. I had those feelings on many occasions.

Some people refer to Barbados as a Caribbean island, but because it is the most easterly of the chain of islands, it is technically in the Atlantic Ocean to the east of the Caribbean Sea and about one hundred miles from the Eastern Caribbean island chain, the Lesser Antilles. Some Bajans have reported that on a clear day when the sea is calm, it is possible to see the outline of the coast of St Lucia from one of the high points in Barbados. I have never experienced such a view, but I travelled to St Lucia in the 1970s and the journey time was so short that we had no sooner settled on the plane than we were preparing to land. The closeness of the island of St Lucia to Barbados is consolidated in my mind because of those trips that I made to St Lucia many years ago. The peculiar location of Barbados makes it complex for ships travelling to the island. There is a saying that when ships are travelling to Barbados, they first sail away from it, then they do a detour to find it.

The climate is subtropical, with the coolest temperatures in February and the warmest temperatures in August. Average temperatures are 26°C (81°F). The dreaded hurricane season extends from July to November. During this period it is possible to experience rain and thunderstorms which can suddenly be replaced by sunny spells. I hated this period when I was a child because of the many occasions on which I was unexpectedly drenched while trying to reach home before the clouds burst and mercilessly delivered torrents of warm water onto frantic fleeing pedestrians. Sometimes the temperature changes considerably at night during the last months of the year. I remember one very cold night when I was at school: many people talked about having to use extra blankets to keep warm, and there were even anecdotal reports of flakes of snow in a parish in the north of the island! The slight variations in temperature are not unbearable, however, and the average Bajan enjoys living on the island and is proud to wave the Bajan flag.

The national flag of Barbados reflects the unadulterated beauty of the island. The flag is comprised of three equal vertical panels. The outer panels are ultramarine and the central panel is gold. There is a black trident with a broken shaft on the central panel. The colour ultramarine represents the blue seas and blue skies that surround the island, the colour gold represents the golden sands that line the beaches, and the black trident represents the mythical sea god Neptune.

There is controversy about the name Barbados. Some believe that Los Barbados was the original name and was of Spanish origin because the Spanish occupied Barbados for a short period from 1492. I studied Spanish at school and always reasoned, like many of my class peers, that the name was of Spanish origin. However, the more plausible explanation offered by the experts is that the Portuguese explorer Pedro a Campos coined the term Los Barbados. The belief is that when the Portuguese first arrived on the island, Pedro a Campos noticed that there was an abundance of fig trees which had long hanging aerial roots that resembled beards, and Los Barbados means 'the bearded ones'. There are other explanations of the origin of the term Los Barbados, including the idea that the foam that sprays the outlying reefs created the image of a beard. The English settlers dropped the prefix Los and simply called the island Barbados after they colonised it. I am often amused when I hear how some Bajans pronounce the word Barbados to sound like 'Bahbaydose'. I often wonder how those Bajans would say 'Los Barbados' if the English had retained the prefix. Why did they drop the prefix in the first place? Was it to rid the island of the Spanish or Portuguese 'taint', or was it to anglicise the name which would in turn rebrand the island as English?

The arrival of the English settlers was the birth of a long historical connection between England and Barbados and brought a complete change in the population. The original natives of Barbados were the Arawak Indians. The Arawak Indians, who were Amerindians from Venezuela, occupied the island around 350 to 400 BC. The belief is that they travelled by dugout canoes from the north end of Venezuela to the Caribbean Sea and eventually to the islands including Barbados. The skill and knowledge of these early inhabitants is a great mystery. How were they able to navigate their journeys across such vast distances? How were they able to cope with the great tidal surges as they paddled in their canoes? Once landed on the island, the Arawak Indians were a peaceable people who were farmers and fishermen. They cultivated cotton, cassava, corn, peanuts, guavas and papaws (papaya).

The Carib Indians conquered the Arawak Indians around the year 1200. The Carib Indians were a pugnacious people. They were taller and stronger than the Arawak Indians and used their arrows and bows with great dexterity and precision. After their defeat of the Arawak Indians, however, the Carib Indians were themselves conquered by the Spanish in 1492. They then met their demise through enslavement and the effects of European diseases like chickenpox and tuberculosis. The Carib Indians became extinct.

Subsequently, Spain began to lose interest in Barbados as they became more enthusiastic about colonising the bigger islands. The bigger islands appeared to have greater potential for profit for the Spaniards, and they eventually abandoned Barbados.

Barbados was colonised by the English around

1625 with the claim that the island was uninhabited when they first arrived in Holetown. Holetown was originally called Jamestown and is on the west coast of Barbados. The settlers claimed the island on behalf of King James I. The English colonial party was comprised of eighty settlers and ten slaves.

Holetown was one of several popular destinations for picnics and excursions when I was a child. It was common practice for churches and individuals to host bus excursions to towns outside Bridgetown. The bus drivers expected the departure and return journey times to be prompt. They were not afraid to show their displeasure if they were asked to wait for 'a few minutes more'. I always felt a buzz of excitement as the excursion date drew closer because there was always a feast waiting to be unloaded and eaten when we reached our destination. The picnic baskets were filled with typical Bajan delicacies like fried and roasted meats, freshly baked bread and cakes, rice, sweet potatoes and other tubers, salads and loads of water, fruit juices, bottled fizzy drinks and mauby. Mauby is a local drink brewed from the bark of the mauby tree (*Colubrina Reclinata*). The brew is flavoured with spices, essence and sugar, is best served with ice cubes and is refreshing especially when drunk on a hot day. The priority after the arrival at the picnic destination was bathroom needs, followed by the feast. There was ample time for the children to play and explore the surrounding area – like one vast playground – and to replenish their energy stores as necessary in between expeditions, while the adults occupied themselves with their own activities. By the end of the day and, more importantly, before sunset, the weary passengers boarded the bus for the home journey with little or no food left in the picnic baskets. I try to visualise what Holetown was like when the first English settlers arrived. No doubt, the sea and the sand were similar to what I saw as a child – blue waters glistening in the sun as the waves continued their restless pursuits, pure clean golden sand that reflected the heat and light of the sun – and the probability is that this same state of affairs will continue when I have left this earth.

Sometime after their arrival, the English settlers persuaded Amerindians from Guiana (Guyana) to come to Barbados. The Amerindians were employed to instruct the English settlers in survival skills, including identifying the local foods, learning how to prepare them and clearing dense tropical forests.

The colonists first developed the cotton and tobacco plantations, but several years later they discovered that the sugar cane had greater potential for profit. They then concentrated on developing the sugar cane crops.

The workers on the plantations were initially white British civilians. Some of the civilians, the indentured servants, signed agreements to work for the plantation owners for a period of five to seven years. After that period they were free of their commitment to the plantation owners. The industries on the island were growing rapidly, however, and the demand for a bigger labour force became apparent. Many white workers were kidnapped in Britain and taken to

Barbados. The kidnapped people included prisoners of war, political dissenters, convicted criminals and women and children. The white slaves, especially the Irish, were treated in the same manner as the black slaves. The white slaves, unlike the white indentured servants, had no hope of freedom. They were regarded as commodities that could be bought and sold; their children were born into hereditary slavery and remained as slaves for the rest of their lives.

The sustained expansion of and demand for sugar created an even greater shortage of workers. The colonial masters enslaved black West Africans to bridge the gap. The African slaves were kidnapped in Sierra Leone, Guinea, Ghana, the Ivory Coast and Cameroon and were transported across the Atlantic Ocean to Barbados, other Caribbean islands and America. They were later sold and resold to slave masters like animal commodities.

The black slaves in Barbados, like the white slaves, were enslaved for life. They lived in very poor conditions and were treated despicably in spite of the wealth that flowed to the plantation owners from the sugar cane industry. The slave masters condoned willing and unwilling sexual unions between the white and black slaves. The offspring of these unions were referred to as 'mulatto' children and were seen by the plantation owners as a potential costless supply of future slave labour.

The influx of the black African slaves, the high mortality of the white slaves and the racial intermixing resulted in a dwindling white population in Barbados. Today there is a minority of white descendants of the white slaves who live in areas like the parish of St Andrew. The typical Bajan is a bubble in the genetic melting pot that is a legacy of slavery. Because of this genetic puzzle, it is difficult for a Bajan to direct any feelings of hatred and anger at any specific group for the suffering of our ancestors.

One of the peculiar features of black families is the colour variation in the offspring. Most Bajan families are comprised of offspring of different shades of black. My family was no exception. The less critically aware individual may question the paternity of a child if the skin colouring is not the expected shade of black. However, as the phenomenon is common amongst most black families, people generally accept the colouring as part of the genetic puzzle. Skin colouring was significant during the era of slavery because a person with a lighter skin colour was treated considerably better than the black slaves. The maltreatment of the black slaves was one of the major factors that led to the slave revolt in 1816.

The slave revolt in 1816 was the catalyst that reduced the harsh treatment of black slaves and subsequently changed the course of the history of slavery in Barbados. A black slave called Bussa led the revolt in protest against the brutality and poor treatment of slaves. The colonial militia extinguished the revolt, but the incident forced the slave masters to begin to improve the conditions and treatment of the slaves.

Slavery was eventually abolished in Barbados in 1834, but this did not bring any immediate tangible benefits to the slaves. They were forced either to continue working on the plantations or to live in shanty towns as they struggled to survive. When I think of my ancestors, it is painful to remember that my great-great-grandparents were slaves who endured humiliation and frustration and died in despair without ever experiencing the benefits of basic human dignity. I am incensed with rage, but realise that the perpetrators of their sad plight are no longer alive. To whom do I direct my anger?

One positive aspect of the abolition of slavery in Barbados, however, was that education became available to the former slaves. Once educated, the former slaves began to aspire to things that were better than working on the plantations. The literacy rate in Barbados in the twenty-first century is exceptional for a developing Third World country. The slaves formally celebrated the abolition of slavery in 1838. Their celebration of freedom is high-lighted in the following folk song:

> Lick an lock-up done wid,
> Hurray fuh Jin-Jin!
> De Queen come from England to set we free
> Now lick an lock-up done wid,
> Hurrah fuh Jin-Jin!

When translated into English, the song is saying that the beatings or whippings and the incarcerations by the slave masters are over and that the queen from England liberated them. The words of this folk song are engraved on the side of the Emancipation Statue in Barbados. The statue was erected to honour the

13

courage and sacrifice of Bussa. He died a hero in the struggle for the freedom of the slaves from the chains of the slave masters. It was surreal when I stood next to the statue, steeped as it is in the dark history of pain and suffering of a people who were placed in a situation over which they had no control. One man, Bussa, was their sacrificial lamb who took away some of the acute pain. Symptoms of that chronic pain still exist in the form of the legacy of slavery.

Remnants of that legacy in Barbados were still very visible when I was a child. Sometimes the term 'African' was used as a derogatory term by some bigots to insult a black Bajan. 'African' was synonymous with 'black', and 'black' was associated with the historical negative connotations of slavery. Some people still judged others by the colour of their skin. A person with a lighter skin tone was preferred by some employers to a darker-skinned person. It was exceptional to see a dark-skinned person working in some of the stores and banks in Bridgetown. A dark-skinned person who was rich (and of the upper class by virtue of his/her wealth) was more easily accepted in the important social circles than a poorer dark-skinned person.

Primary education in Barbados was free and available to every child, but free secondary or high school education was a lottery: children whose parents were connected by virtue of their social status were better placed to gain entry to the top high schools. The eventual outcome of the children from those schools was potentially better than that of the average secondary or high school graduate. Many

14

parents were forced to pay for their children to receive secondary or high school education. My parents were not of 'high' social status and therefore paid for my siblings and me to be educated after the compulsory free primary education. It was no mean feat for them as they struggled to pay school fees every term. I knew that they were making a great sacrifice in the interest of our education. My awareness of that sacrifice was a factor that motivated me to strive to achieve the most that I could at high school.

Emigration, immigration and the existing equity and equality in educational opportunities for all children in Barbados have lightened the burden of the slave legacy and removed some of the shackles that impeded the progress of the people and the island for such a long time. There is still much to be done to eradicate this awful dark legacy, however.

Barbados was under British rule from the seventeenth century until 30 November 1966, when it became an independent state within the Commonwealth of Nations. Queen Elizabeth II remains the head of state and is represented in Barbados by the Governor General. Prior to independence in 1966, Barbados was an internal self-governing country from 1961 to 1966.

The population of Barbados is about 260,000, with a stable democratic government. The official language is English and the local dialect is Bajan, a language that was created by combining West African and English speech. During my childhood we were barred from speaking the Bajan dialect because it was perceived to be associated with people of lower intelligence or status. Schools emphasised speaking proper English, but we spoke Bajan amongst our peers and at home. As an adult I am proud to speak Bajan when I am socialising with other Bajans.

The natives of Barbados are also called Bajans. They are mainly descendants of black West African slaves, white Europeans (mostly Scots and Irish slaves) and Amerindians. They live a largely sedate life immersed in an eclectic culture that has evolved over the centuries.

Barbados trades mainly with other Caribbean islands, Britain and the USA, and the largest exports are sugar and molasses. Molasses was a treat for me and my siblings during the sugar cane harvest. It has a very sticky texture and is very dark in colour. We liked to add it to drinks or fruit and even sago porridge.

Barbados is a popular tourist attraction because of its geographical location and physical beauty. It has a large tourist industry and a manufacturing industry that is involved with chemicals, electrical components, clothing and rum. I worked briefly as a nurse attached to the health department at the Barbados Seawell airport (now called the Grantley Adams airport) in the 1970s. It was an amazing experience to see the constant streams of tourists passing through the immigration department every week – and the number of tourists visiting Barbados in the twenty-first century has increased considerably.

The unit of currency is the Barbados (BDS) dollar. One BDS dollar is equal to 100 cents. In my school days we were taught the imperial pounds, shillings and pence system, where 20 shillings were equal to one pound, as well as the dollars and cents system. We were also familiar with the metric system of francs and centimes. Knowledge of the imperial system was beneficial to me when I came to England in the 1960s, as I immediately came to terms with using the British currency.

There is a strong Christian tradition on the island, although other religions are also represented. The Anglican Church's influence is reflected in the names of the eleven regions or parishes of Barbados, and each has an Anglican parish church.

Other examples of English influence are seen in the names of some of the places, including Hastings, Yorkshire, Worthing and Greenwich. The striking similarities of some aspects of the island with those of England earned it the name 'Little England' for many decades. The name is not as appropriate now as it was before independence, nor would the innuendo implied by the name be as hurtful to some Bajans as it was decades ago. At the same time, some Bajans were very enthusiastic about the title and perceived it as a positive reflection of being in synchrony with the colonial 'mother country'. Conversely, the enthusiasm would not now be as marked as it was before independence.

Barbados in the twenty-first century is undoubtedly more developed than it was in 1966, but its beauty, culture, government and the friendly attitude of the people remain the same as they were in 1966 and before. I am always impressed by the general attitude of Bajans to giving directions to tourists. I am particularly proud of the way in which they help expatriate Bajans who return to the island. It is easy for the expatriates to become confused or lost because of the variety of developments that have taken place during the years that they have been away from the island. It is not even unusual for a school child to give clear and precise directions to any person who enquires about a particular location in Barbados. Bajans are well versed in the history and geography of the island and exude pride in being Bajan. For myself, pride in my Bajan origins increased after the island gained its independence.

The year 1966 is of great significance to me because it was during that year – as a teenager barely out of school – that I made the bold step to immigrate to England. It was also the year that Barbados gained its independence from Britain. I was heartbroken that I was not able to participate in the independence celebrations in Barbados in November 1966, but I tried to be objective about my situation. I was an independent teenager with an opportunity to become whatever I wanted to be, and my country Barbados was an independent island with the potential to become whatever the people and the government wanted it to be.

I had no fear of travelling to England to study because I was the holder of a valid passport with the words 'BRITISH PASSPORT, BARBADOS' on the front cover and my national status was listed as 'BRITISH SUBJECT: CITIZEN OF THE UNITED KINGDOM AND COLONIES' on the first page.

Armed with my British passport, dressed in formal

attire as the trend was then, and feeling confident that I would adapt easily to the British way of life, I took the bold step to leave the island for the 'mother country', England.

On a warm sunny evening, Thursday 16 June 1966, I boarded an aeroplane bound for London Heathrow airport. The flight distance between Barbados and London is about 4,207 air miles (6,771 air kilometres) and the flight duration is about eight hours. The flight stopped briefly at another West Indian island, Antigua, which is about 314 miles (505 kilometres) from Barbados, before continuing the rest of the transatlantic journey to London.

I left the land of my birth as a young Bajan teenager whose view of life was tainted in some respects by naivety, that beautiful force called teenage optimism (bordering on over-optimism) and my limited knowledge of the mother country.

The Arrival

It was a bleak day in June 1966 when the BOAC (British Overseas Airways Corporation) plane landed at Heathrow airport in London, England. The air was moist and there was a grey mist hanging over the tarmac. The skies were grey as dark clouds hung threateningly over the land. I felt utter panic as an overwhelming homesickness engulfed my entire body. My thoughts were racing and tears filled my eyes. *Is this the England that I have been dreaming of for so many months?* I felt utter disappointment at what I saw and wished that I could clamber back on to the plane and fly away to the sunshine island that I had left just eight hours before. *Help us, God,* I prayed. *Please help us.*

There were three other young women of my age group who were en route to the same hospital as I was, to train as nurses. They appeared to be as shocked as I was by the surroundings, but managed to smile as we prepared to plant our feet on English soil for the first time. During my early years in England they were my main source of friendship, support and comfort.

I emerged from the aircraft with faltering steps and gingerly placed my feet on the wet tarmac. I boarded a bus with the other passengers and reached the terminal after a few minutes. I later discovered that the 'bus' was called a 'coach'. This was the first of so many differences, big and small.

I followed the other passengers through immigration and control. This was a painfully slow process that accentuated my fatigue and my feelings of utter despair. After what seemed like an eternity, I emerged into a large open area where representatives from the British Council welcomed me. They seemed to be professional as they explained to me that I would travel to the British Rail King's Cross station by taxi. From King's Cross I would take the train to Wakefield Westgate station in Yorkshire, a county in the northern region of England about 220 miles (352 kilometres) from London. There would be a tutor from the hospital waiting to meet me at Wakefield Westgate station and take me to the nurses' home. The nurses' home, I thought grudgingly, would be my home for a very long time. I prayed again, *God, please help us.*

The taxi ride from Heathrow to King's Cross was a monotonous, bleak affair. Everything looked grey – the skies, the streets and the people as they hurried through the streets, wearing mainly black and white clothes. *Why is there no colour to this place?* I thought. *Why do people look so sad? Why no smiles? Why are there so many factories?*

During my first week in England, I discovered that the buildings I had perceived to be factories were not factories at all. The smoke that I thought was coming from factories was in fact coming from the chimneys of the houses where people were burning coal in their fireplaces in order to keep warm. Most people had no other form of heating in those days. When it came to the freezing cold of winter, we heard of people suffering from frostbite and even hypothermia, leading to eventual death.

There was a fine spattering of raindrops that bounced off the windshield of the taxi as it travelled at a moderate pace through the streets of London. I could hear the taxi driver speaking, but I was not really interested in talking. I just wanted to feel miserable all on my own. The three other young ladies, who were travelling in the same taxi, took turns at responding to the taxi driver and I was grateful that I did not have to make any effort to join in. They spoke on my behalf and I did not mind at all.

The four of us had met about six weeks before our departure for England and had formed a sort of bond. We realised then that we would have to be surrogate sisters to each other in order to survive in the new country. That period of time before our departure was occupied with medical examinations, immunisations and vaccinations – and yes, those injections were brutal. I felt ill for about a week after the injections. My arm ached, my body ached, and even my brain felt as though it was in pain. During that week after the injections, I spent many days sitting in the sunshine in Barbados because I felt so cold. On reflection now, I realise that compared to my early days in England, the suffering from the injections was a transient, insignificant, trivial irritation!

Viv was the mother of the group. She was twenty years old then. She told me that she was the youngest of four children and had one brother and two sisters. She was, however, the oldest in our group. Viv naturally assumed the role of surrogate mother, especially to me. I guessed that one of the reasons for her protective attitude towards me was that prior to our leaving Barbados she had made a promise to my parents that as she was older, she would look after me. Forty years later, Viv has not changed. We are still very good friends and although we communicate infrequently, the relationship that we had so many years ago is still flourishing – perhaps because we have grown older and wiser.

Gwen was the next oldest. She told me that she was the oldest of her siblings. Although she was the quiet one in the group, she possessed a wealth of experience and always had a common-sense approach to problem solving.

Diana was the optimist. She had a ready smile and made light of difficult situations when things were not going so well for us. She was not backward in coming forward, as the saying goes. She was pleasantly assertive. She told me that she was the youngest of her siblings.

I was the baby of the group and although I have never said it before, I appreciated the protective attitude of the others towards me. I was the second child as well as the second daughter, out of seven children. My parents had six daughters and one son. My brother was in the middle of three older sisters and three younger sisters. My parents were always

24

there for us when we were growing up. My mother was a traditional housewife and my father was an electrician. In addition to his main job, he dabbled in plumbing and stone masonry. You could say that he was a jack-of-all-trades. He had the uncanny ability to fix anything, no matter how complex it appeared to us. My parents sacrificed the luxuries of life to ensure that we were well fed and clothed and our school fees were paid every term. Friday, my father's pay day, was 'special treat' day for the whole family. My mother was usually as excited as we were. My father arrived home in the evening laden with bags of fruit, nuts, sweets, popcorn and other goodies. It was the only day in the week when my mother did not cook supper. After gorging ourselves on the treats, we would sit around chatting about the week at school and work until bedtime.

My mother was an excellent cook and, like many other Bajan wives and mothers at the time, seemed to spend most of her day preparing fresh, nutritious meals. My mother's task was compounded by her having to feed my father and seven of us at least three times a day. She rarely expressed any feelings of frustration with the long day in the kitchen, but I am sure that she must have been exhausted on some occasions. My mother was a Christian woman who married at the age of twenty-one. She practised what she preached and used her religious beliefs to help her through the day. Meals were delicious and usually included some type of meat, be it pork, poultry, lamb or beef, and fish, especially the Bajan fish, the flying fish. Sunday was our special feast day.

The feast always followed our Sunday morning visit to church. There were also large helpings of rice and peas coated with hot spicy gravy and decorated with freshly made salad. We usually washed the food down with ice-cold drinks like freshly made lemonade or some of the other fizzy drinks like Ju-C. This drink was better known to us as 'Juicy' and was an extra treat. After the feast we relaxed listening to music, hearing stories, reading or generally lazing around. Sometimes we snoozed. We jokingly referred to this phenomenon as 'black man's syndrome', that is, sleep after filling the stomach.

Our upbringing was moderately religious. We attended church twice on Sundays. On Sunday morning we went to our mother's church. She was of the 'free church' orientation. On Sunday afternoon we attended our father's church. My father was a confirmed devout Anglican who prided himself on having been an altar boy during his childhood. Sundays were enjoyable days, though. It was the one day of the week when we were able to dress in our best dresses, shoes and ribbons. It was heavenly walking to church in the sunshine. It was doom and gloom during the rainy season, though, because we believed that there was nothing worse than arriving at church with muddy shoes and wet white socks, and it was one sure way of dampening the excitement of going to church.

Sunday evenings were spent completing homework and reading books and newspapers. My parents attached much value to reading. We spent a great amount of our time visiting the library and borrowing books. At home we were always competing to see who could finish a book first. Books were not plentiful because of the high demand of other Bajan children on the library resources. To overcome the shortage, my siblings and I exchanged books as soon as we finished reading them and in so doing could easily finish five books each before the due date of return to the library. Reading is a skill which is best developed in early childhood. The skill is a valuable tool which has a place in all aspects of life. It was undoubtedly useful to me during my studies, my working life and as a hobby.

I feel that I was able to survive in England and in the nursing profession mainly because of the secure family environment that I enjoyed during the first eighteen years of my life. I was able to draw on the inner strength that I had mustered from the upbringing that my parents provided for me during my formative years.

I always wanted to become a nurse. My parents wanted me to become a secretary because many parents, including mine, saw nursing as a 'dirty job'. One defining aspect of my desire to become a nurse was the observations that I made on the occasional visits I made to the emergency room of the Barbados General Hospital. I seemed to be accident-prone in my early years and frequently sustained cuts and bruises. My mother was always alert to getting me to Casualty, as it was called in those days. The main purpose was for me to get the tetanus injection: she was not prepared to let me get 'lockjaw'. I was always impressed by the way in which the nurses carried out their duties. Naturally, the caring attitude of the nurses moderated the pain of the anti-tetanus injections.

When I was about eighteen years old, a chance encounter with a man who was involved in a road traffic accident consolidated my resolve to become a nurse. It was on a warm sunny afternoon when I was slowly walking from school to my home, about a mile away. About ten minutes after leaving my school, I began the slow climb up Government Hill Road. The road was mostly a steep hill that ran adjacent to Government House. On the left of the road when travelling in a northerly direction was a long row of houses and on the right was a wall, many metres high and bordering the rear grounds of Government House. Government House was originally the residence of the Queen's representative. In 1966, when Barbados became an independent country, it became the residence of the Governor General of Barbados.

I was recovering from the exertion of the climb as the hill levelled out, when I noticed a gathering of people on the edge of a side road that joined Government Hill Road. Sitting on the ground with his back to a wall was a young man with blood streaming down his fingers. The blood was settling in a tiny pool on the ground. The young man was in a state of shock as he fixed his gaze on his bleeding hand. There was another agitated young man who was going around in circles pleading with the crowd to believe that he had tried his best to avoid the crash. I inferred from the behaviour that he was the driver of the crashed vehicle and the young man with the bleeding hand was a passenger in the same car. Although someone in the crowd had summoned the emergency services which included the ambulance and the police, no one was making any effort to help the injured man.

I was at that time a member of the Junior Red Cross Society and had acquired basic first aid skills at the group meetings at school. These skills included stopping haemorrhage and applying bandages to wounds. I felt compelled to offer some assistance. I told the young man my name and explained that I was a member of the Junior Red Cross Society. I offered to help to stop the bleeding. He told me his name, but here I shall refer to him as David. One of the people in the crowd provided some cloth that was the nearest thing to a bandage we could find. I applied the cloth to the site that appeared to be the cause of the bleeding. I then asked David to raise his arm. I had learned from the first aid instructor that elevation of a limb would help to stem the flow of blood. As the blood flow duly diminished, David became calmer. A short time later the emergency services arrived and took control of the situation. I quietly slipped away from the scene after saying goodbye to David.

I did not expect to see David again and it was therefore a pleasant surprise, some weeks later, to encounter him once more. He was fully recovered from the accident and expressed his gratitude for the help that I had offered. I learned from him that the police department was conducting enquiries into the cause of the accident.

I told David that his unfortunate accident had helped me to decide to become a nurse and that I was making applications to study nursing. He was overjoyed at my decision and showered me with torrents of good wishes. Several months later I was on a passenger plane bound for England and a totally new experience.

I had spent several summer holidays away from home at youth camps or with school friends, but I had never travelled abroad before. Many of my school friends said that I was brave to embark on such a drastic change. There were opportunities for me to study nursing in Barbados, but it was as though I had to answer a call to leave Barbados to study nursing in a foreign country: unless I answered that call I would always regret missing the opportunity.

My mother was quietly supportive of my decision and assisted me with most of the preparations for travel. She reminded me of the importance of a prayerful, God-fearing commitment to all of my undertakings after I arrived in England. She told me that she would continue to pray for me, but that I would also have to pray on my own behalf. My father was also quietly overjoyed that I decided to study in England. He had several reasons for wanting me to study there. He was a product of the *Windrush* era and had worked in Birmingham for the British Railways during the 1950s.

The *Windrush* was synonymous with the first generation of Caribbean migrant workers who came to Britain in the post-Second World War years. The SS *Empire Windrush* was built in Germany, a steamship designed to carry tourists. She was originally called *Monte Rosa* and sailed between Hamburg and Buenos Aires in Argentina. During the Second World War the ship was converted into a troop carrier, and later a hospital ship. After the defeat of the Germans, the British forces seized the ship at Kiel in Germany. She became a British troop carrier and was renamed the *Empire Windrush* in 1947.

In 1948, when the *Empire Windrush* was sailing from Australia to the Tilbury docks in Essex, England, it berthed at Kingston, Jamaica, in order to pick up the first West Indian migrant workers. The migrants had responded to an advert which appeared in a local Jamaican paper in April 1948. The advert invited responses from persons who were interested in working in the United Kingdom. Most of the West Indians who responded were ex-service personnel who had contributed to the Second World War effort. Motivating factors included a desire to continue to work in the services and to visit the 'mother country'. The migrants were subsequently dispersed to the National Health Service, the mills, London Transport and other seemingly appropriate employment.

There was debate in the British parliament at that time about the appropriateness of the West Indian migrants coming to Britain, but the overriding factor was that the migrants possessed British passports and therefore should not be barred. The *Windrush* migrants were initially housed in war shelters in south-west London. As immigration increased, the dispersal of the workers was extended to other counties and countries in Britain. This first group of migrants are seen as the pioneers of West Indian migration to Britain.

The SS *Empire Windrush* met its demise in an explosion in 1954 on a journey from Japan to Southampton. Fortunately the passengers escaped with their lives, but the disaster claimed the lives of four of the ship's engineers. Migration continued in other vessels, of course, and my father was among the travellers.

The saying, 'There is an ill wind that blows nobody any good,' was apt for my father and his decision to travel to England. My father's journey resulted from acute need that was a consequence of a natural disaster, Hurricane Janet. He spent about one year in England and returned to Barbados late in 1956.

In September 1955 Barbados was devastated by Hurricane Janet, a Category 3 hurricane. My parents were fortunate because our house was still habitable at the end of the disaster, despite the widespread devastation on the island. I was seven years old at the time, but I can still hear the wind and feel the stinging rain on my face as we struggled to reach the hurricane shelter. The wind was like a strong hand that kept pushing me back. It was so strong that it lifted skirts high above heads and converted them into blindfolds. Wearing a hat was a waste of time because hats and caps were ripped off as if an invisible hand was flicking them in the air and whisking them away at supersonic speed. Somehow, in the race to the shelter, I quickly adapted to the force by crouching low as we struggled to walk the quarter of a mile to safety. My mother lost one of her shoes, but she did not even attempt to retrieve it.

When the hurricane had completely swept over the island, there was an eerie calm. I heard my parents saying that Barbados was hit by the tail end of the hurricane and that if the island had been hit by the full force of the hurricane not many buildings would have been left intact and loss of life might have been more extensive. I remember several adults and children huddled together with anxiety and fear etched on their faces. I was petrified as well. Some adults were on their knees praying, some just sat staring ahead. The children sat around bewildered by the roar of the wind, but still oblivious to the real danger of the hurricane.

The aftermath was one of utter devastation. Thirty-five people lost their lives and about twenty thousand were left homeless. Hurricane San Calixto II was the deadliest recorded hurricane in Bajan history. It hit Barbados in 1780 and more than four thousand people lost their lives. Hurricane Janet was, by comparison, only moderately destructive in terms of the loss of life.

In spite of the chaos that resulted from Hurricane Janet, some people were still able to cook a meal. I remember eating boiled rice topped with corn beef that had been served straight from the can. The important thing was that stomachs were not empty, especially when there was news that the hurricane might return to the island. The islanders breathed a sigh of relief when the all-clear was given.

Several days later we were able to return to our

home. It was damaged, but still habitable. Several houses nearby were roofless, others had missing windows or doors and some were completely obliterated. I always pray that I will never experience another hurricane, but unfortunately hurricanes in the Caribbean are part of the annual weather cycle with a yearly period of anxiety for all islanders in the region between June and October.

My experience of the hurricane was the most traumatic event that I have ever endured. I have been told that war is just as traumatic as a hurricane – although a hurricane is usually over in hours, whereas war may last for weeks or years. Still, in both of these tragedies, the aftermath is usually seen in human suffering, both short and long-term, and often involving fatalities and serious consequences for the survivors.

Some people never totally recover from such trauma, some recover partially and the lucky ones experience complete recovery. I rate myself as having partly recovered, as the thought of hurricanes still fills me with fear. Although our house was habitable, it was still very difficult for everyone in our household. Our parents tried to forage for themselves and five children: one of us was under five years old and my mother was heavily pregnant. Her sixth child, another daughter, was born in November of the same year.

Life was a struggle after the hurricane and many adults talked about going abroad to England to work in order to earn money to help rebuild their lives and the lives of their families. My father was no exception, and in 1956 he travelled to Birmingham, England, to work with the British Railways.

When I was contemplating travelling in 1966, I felt somehow that he wanted me to go to England to gain experience of working in a totally different country, even though my type of employment would be different in many respects from his own. Maybe he hoped that I would complete the dream that he had wanted to fulfil during his time in England.

My father gave me some advice about surviving there. He told me about the freezing winter temperatures and the need to wear warm clothing. He also told me a lot about feeling homesick. I wondered if the reason for his early return to Barbados in the 1950s was that he had missed us and my mother too much. He told me about the trains and his job as a guard, and leaving home to go to work on dark winter days when the sun did not rise until late morning. This was very different from Barbados, where sunrise is around six in the morning and sunset around six in the evening. The idea that it might still be dark in the early morning was very strange to me.

The Barbados government financed my airfare, but I had to agree to repay them the total cost, starting as soon as possible during my first year in England. It was standard practice then for the government to assist migrants with their airfare if they or their families were unable to meet the costs.

An important requirement was that all candidates should have guarantors. The guarantors were land-owners who had to use their land as surety against the loan. Traditionally Bajans attach great significance to landownership and it is not uncommon for plots of land to be passed on from one generation to another. My family maintained such a tradition, so my father and my uncle Eustace acted as my guarantors. They used our family's land as surety.

As soon as I started earning money in England, I made regular repayments towards the loan in Barbados. The salary for a trainee nurse was about eleven pounds sterling per month in the late 1960s. By today's standards that was a tidy sum of money for an eighteen-year-old.

During my first two years in England, I was able to live comfortably on the nurse's salary. I bought essential items for myself every month and saved most of the money. I even managed a student budget trip abroad. I travelled with Viv to an international centre in West Germany. The centre existed to cater for people like students. Amenities were basic, but the food was delicious and the bunk beds were clean and comfortable.

I was able to repay all of the cost of the airfare to the Barbados government by the end of my second year in England. This was a great relief for my family and me.

All that lay ahead of me, however, on that first rainy day in England. The journey from King's Cross to Wakefield was surreal. I had never travelled by train before. There were no trains in Barbados. Bajans travelled around the island on foot, by bicycle, motorcycle, car or bus, or in a horse-drawn cart. We were on board a 'slow train' that chugged and chugged its way north. It passed through wide open spaces, then suddenly zipped past houses, or fields with cattle grazing. Sometimes the cattle looked like toy animals on a dark green cloth in the distance.

My companions and I took turns at keeping watch or sleeping, although we were aware that the train was terminating at Wakefield so we were in no danger of missing our stop. We wanted to be awake when we arrived, but we were overwhelmed by fatigue from the long haul over the Atlantic Ocean. On several occasions we were all awake simultaneously and made light conversation, commenting on things like the gloomy June day and our fears of training to be nurses in a foreign country. It was then that we pledged to support each other in our new environment, in spite of any challenges that might present themselves.

The name Yorkshire had a familiar ring to it. There is a place in Barbados called Yorkshire, in the countryside about ten miles from the capital, Bridgetown. My recollection of the road from Bridgetown to Yorkshire is quite clear. It started as a crowded shopping centre. About four miles from Bridgetown, the road became more deserted, with less bustle, a more sporadic stream of traffic, the occasional bicyclist or motorcyclist, the odd slow-moving horse-drawn cart, and houses dotted along the route. The houses were sometimes miles apart, but occasionally there was a small cluster. There were some grocery stores as well, some rum shops and the odd gas station. Then the road to Yorkshire suddenly changed to a mainly clear route with a vast sea of sugar cane fields all around, the cane plants gently moving in the breeze on a clear sunny day. Sometimes there was the smell of the sugar cane juice being processed in the sugar factory in the distance and imaginary droplets of cane juice touched my palate as I inhaled the nectar-like scent.

My arrival in Yorkshire, England, on Friday 17 June 1966 was nothing like I had imagined. I was in a state of detached consciousness when the train jolted to a stop at the station. I jumped up from my seat when I heard a voice over a loudspeaker bellowing, 'This is Wakefield, Westgate!' I scrambled to collect my luggage from the rack in the carriage and noticed that Viv, Diana and Gwen were tripping over each other as they tried to exit the train and make it onto the platform. Then we just stood there trying to make sense of the unfamiliar scene.

A station guard immediately recognised us as 'new blood'. We stood out like sore thumbs. He approached us and enquired if we had come to train as nurses in the local hospital. It appeared to be the established notion that most non-white persons worked either in the health professions or in the transport industry. The station guard was a kindly looking middle-aged man, and after we had explained that we were scheduled to meet a tutor from the hospital, he escorted us to the station lobby. He showed us the waiting room and suggested that we rested there until the tutor arrived. We seemed to wait for an eternity. Apathy eventually turned to concern when the tutor still had not appeared.

We were debating what our next course of action

should be when a young black man approached us. He told us his name, explained that he was African and was a student at the local university. I will call him Tunde. Within fifteen minutes of meeting us, Tunde had contacted the hospital and put us in a taxi. Tunde remained our friend during our time in Wakefield and often visited us to enquire about our progress. In fact, he was our surrogate father, but he never imposed himself on us. We always expressed our gratitude to him for rescuing us. I left Wakefield two years later to continue nursing studies in Nottinghamshire, and although I maintained contact with Viv, Diana and Gwen, unfortunately I never saw Tunde again.

The taxi had no sooner parked outside the nurses' quarters than the nurse tutor parked her small car behind us and rushed to meet us. She apologised profusely for not being at the station. There had been some confusion about our arrival time. After paying the taxi driver, the tutor introduced herself as our course tutor. We told her our names, which she already knew, although she had to marry a face to each name. As we continued with the introductions, a group of maids suddenly appeared at the entrance to the nurses' quarters as if on cue. They were dressed in dark brown dresses decorated with crisp white aprons. Tiny frilly caps sat precariously on their heads and friendly beaming smiles lit up their faces. We returned their smiles even though we were on the brink of collapse from fatigue. They were brisk and efficient as they helped us with our luggage up two flights of stairs. They deposited each piece of luggage in the appropriate room and left us to settle in. We were scheduled to have a meal within an hour of our arrival.

My room was like all the other rooms in the nurses' quarters. It was the epitome of utility. The door to the room opened onto a long corridor. Immediately inside the room there was a single bed and a wardrobe, one on either side of the room. The bed was covered with two clean crisp white sheets. The bottom sheet covered the mattress and the top sheet was tucked in at the foot of the bed over the bottom sheet. A set of blankets was laid over the top sheet, which was folded back over the blankets and tucked in on either side of the mattress. Two white pillows, covered by a set of pillowcases, completed the lower layers. A coloured bedspread was draped over the top. A chest of drawers with an attached single hinged mirror was at the far end of the room. A single straight-backed chair, an easy chair and a laundry basket completed the arrangement. A single window opened onto the long drive and its spacious surroundings. The room was my only haven of solace and privacy for two years. This type of room arrangement was not peculiar to the nurses' quarters in Wakefield, because I encountered similar arrangements in other settings when I undertook further nursing courses.

Wakefield is located in the heart of England in West Yorkshire. The cathedral church of All Saints has Yorkshire's tallest spire at 83 metres. All Saints is a fifteenth-century church and was made a cathedral in 1888. Wakefield was a medieval weaving centre and was the chief Yorkshire cloth town for about 700 years until the seventeenth century, when trade was taken over by the Bradford and Leeds mills. In medieval times Wakefield was referred to as 'The Merrie City' and the famous Wars of the Roses and the English Civil War featured in this area of Yorkshire. Some believe that Robin Hood, who is associated with Sherwood Forest in Nottinghamshire, may have been a man called Robert Hode, a native of Wakefield. The famous hymn 'Onward Christian Soldiers' was apparently written as a processional song for the children of Horbury Bridge, Wakefield, in the nineteenth century.

Wakefield in the twenty-first century is completely different from the Wakefield of the 1960s that I can recall so clearly. In 1966 miners came straight from the pits and made their way home through the town with coal-blackened faces and dirty overalls and boots. In those days I was reminded of a popular television musical or comedy called *The Black and White Minstrels Show* whenever I saw the pale-coloured eyes piercing through the coal-blackened faces. Things changed considerably over the years as the coal mining industry in England declined and more emphasis was placed on health and safety issues, including hygiene for the workers.

The training hospital where I gained my early experiences of nursing was opened in 1933 with an original complement of 103 beds. It was a gift to the community from a local benefactor. The hospital was later vested in the Secretary of State under the National Health Service Act 1946, free of any trust.

The hospital site was comprised of several single units that were situated at reasonable distances apart. The nurses' quarters and other service units that included the boiler house were in the centre of the grounds. The boiler house was crucial to a continuous supply of hot water, as well as providing heat for the hospital complex during the cold winter months, which in Yorkshire frequently reached temperatures below freezing point. The lawns and flower gardens were well maintained and summer days were graced with an array of colourful flowers and rainbows of bedding plants. A high wrought-iron gate guarded the entrance to the hospital. The hospital lodge was on the right very close to the entrance and a clean, medium-sized path stretched over the distance of the site with side paths leading to the various buildings in the complex. The hospital lodge was the security site and was the first port of call for all visitors, irrespective of status. The gates were controlled by the gatekeeper who was also a porter. The gates were closed at night for security purposes. To gain entry at night, all visitors had to be screened, and that included nurses. The porters were multifunctional as their tasks included transport of patients, meals, laundry and communication, amongst others. The porters were seen as part of the establishment who should be respected equally with others like nurses and doctors and they played a significant role in patient care.

Caring for patients was central to training as a nurse. In the early days I found my training fraught with minor and major frustrations on the wards as well as in the nurses' accommodation block. Many trainee nurses lived in the on-site nurses' residence, which was called the 'nurses' home'.

My first experience of such frustration was on a day during the second week after I arrived in Yorkshire. The 'new girls', meaning the four new student nurses who had just arrived from the West Indies, were summoned to the matron's office. We were trembling with anxiety because the matron instilled fear in all hospital workers, be they porters, nurses, patients or doctors. She summoned people to her office usually when there was a problem; on rare occasions it was when there was something positive to communicate. We reasoned that we had not been in England long enough to merit any positive feedback, therefore we were in deep trouble.

We discovered that the matron had received a complaint that the new nurses were causing a disturbance because they were bathing very early in the morning and the noise from the bathroom was disturbing others who were trying to sleep. This was a great shock to the four of us because it was a routine part of the Bajan culture to take a shower early in the morning. This was an essential element of the morning ablutions. Failure to shower was tantamount to failure to brush one's teeth on waking in the morning, or having breakfast without brushing one's teeth. Most Bajans take showers at least twice every day because of the hot climate.

We explained our reason for the early morning ablutions and the matron advised us to avoid these early activities or be quieter when performing our ablutions. After what seemed like the scolding of children by a mother, we gathered in my room to lick our wounds. We were angry, tearful and traumatised by the experience. We talked for hours about our feelings and of the apparent pettiness of the complaint, but realised that much was demanded of us by our parents, families, friends and our country Barbados. We had no other option than to endure the hurt and plod on even when we felt wounded. A wave of homesickness overwhelmed me and if it were possible then to return to Barbados, I would have done so, but like my other three friends I vowed to continue the struggle amid a torrent of tears.

As the weeks and months passed, we were able to adjust to the needs of the other nurses and tempered the intensity of our morning ablutions, especially during the cold winter months. We were able to explain to them the rationale for our early morning baths and they eventually forgave us for our earlier transgressions. By that time, we were accustomed to having meaningful interaction and communication with our Yorkshire colleagues, especially the indigenous Yorkshire lasses. This was a major hurdle for me because the communication setbacks that I had experienced early on were still dancing in my subconscious mind.

Verbal communication during the early months in Yorkshire was one of the major frustrations that added to my feelings of homesickness and isolation. I felt that in order to progress with the nurse training I would need to find solutions to the communication barrier that was patently obvious to me. I was acutely aware of the barrier, even though I was fluent in English and was convinced that I was speaking in a grammatically correct way.

Overcoming Barriers

'Where are you from, luv?' asked the elderly man in the middle bed on the right side of the Victorian ward.

'I am from Barbados,' I replied.

'Oh, is Barbados in Jamaica?' he continued.

'No, Barbados is a separate island in the West Indies,' I explained.

'Oh, I thought Barbados was part of Jamaica,' he retorted rather disappointedly.

My first two weeks in Yorkshire were a mixture of bewilderment, disappointment and general shell shock. These emotions left me feeling as though I was on the outside looking in on an unfolding drama. I was disappointed that people like the elderly man in the Victorian ward were unaware of the location of Barbados. I was bewildered because the history that was taught at school in Barbados impressed upon us the importance of learning about England, the mother country; yet some people in the mother country were not even aware of the location of my island or how the natives of my country lived, considering that many West Indians had made costly contributions on behalf of the mother country in the great wars.

Some of the patients were old enough to have fought in the wars themselves and would undoubtedly have fought alongside some West Indians and other soldiers from the colonies. I mused that people like the man in the Victorian ward may not have considered that it was important to learn about their comrades from outside the United Kingdom because they were natives of Great Britain and they were the keepers of the power base.

Those first few weeks in Yorkshire were filled with constant questions from patients about the West Indies and Africa. I was unsure whether the questions were based on ignorance or indifference. 'Do they still wear grass skirts in your country?' 'Do they still swing in trees in your country?' 'Do they still live in tree houses in your country, luv?'

I was particularly disappointed and frustrated as I struggled to acclimatise to the culture, the surroundings and the absence of black people. I hated England, Great Britain, the United Kingdom, Wakefield, Yorkshire and everything British. It was a situation of being caught up between a rock and a hard place. My initial impression of the England about which I had romanticised for so many years was one of utter desperation. My dark mood was compounded by the foul, dreary weather that I had experienced on my first day in England. I wondered if things might have been different if the weather had been bright and sunny when I first arrived. The sadness was exacerbated by the knowledge that there was not even a remote possibility of my returning to Barbados at that time, because I had signed a contract to train as a nurse.

It was extremely difficult for me to come to terms with my plight. I was an eighteen-year-old West Indian whose life so far had revolved around school, church and peer activities in a carefree environment. Urged on by the innocence of youth, I had travelled away from my home – to become immersed in alien activities in an unfamiliar country. I had to make adult choices, and on top of that the demands of nursing people and studying was another new phenomenon for me, a mere frightened teenager. I was engulfed in homesickness, faced with the stark reality of being trapped in a tunnel, having to stay in this one institution for more than two years. I had to put away childish ideas and think like an adult. That was the only safe route to the end of the tunnel and freedom. I had to create new survival strategies.

There were other disappointments and feelings of profound bewilderment during those early months in Yorkshire. I was dumbfounded when I travelled on a double-decker bus to see passengers spitting on the floor. It was even more disgusting in the winter months when bronchitis was not uncommon. The consistency of the expectorated material that landed on the floor of the bus was beyond belief. This activity appeared to be a normal occurrence of everyday life and was further compounded by the smoke-filled bus. Smoking on buses was freely allowed at that time, as concerns about the health and safety of passengers was not even in the embryonic stage. As I acquired more nursing knowledge about the potential health risks associated with smoking and spitting, I made a conscious effort to avoid the more smoked-filled areas and tread carefully through the minefield of phlegm grenades whenever I had no option but to travel on the bus. Travelling on the train, by comparison, was not as problematic because of the compartmentalisation of the carriages and the fact that some of the carriages were exclusive to passengers who did not smoke.

It was also alien to me to observe women, especially young women, smoking cigarettes in public. The culture of smoking amongst women was not tolerated in Barbados because women who smoked were presumed to be women of ill repute; smoking was a man's thing. I was aware that some decent, morally conscious Bajan women smoked, but the habit was confined to the secrecy of their own homes. Still, it was a culture shock for me to be offered cigarettes publicly by some of my young nursing colleagues. I realised that the gesture was part of the Yorkshire culture and was a way of being friendly, but I never accepted any of their offers because it was abominable to me. I acquired the skill of responding with a polite 'No thank you' whenever I heard the words 'Have a fag, luv' or 'Do you want a fag, luv?'

I spent many hours reflecting on the other things that were contributing to my frustration apart from bus travel, and realised that I had to learn to ignore those things that I perceived to be major trials. Instead, I should think of them as a minor part of a transient phase in my life. There was an urgent need for me to look beyond those irritations in order to avoid a miserable existence. I had to learn to be at peace with myself first in order to achieve my prime objective of becoming a nurse.

By the middle of the summer of 1966 my mood lightened as I started to enjoy the warm Yorkshire sunshine and admire nature at its best with the beautiful greens and the bright array of flowers. People around appeared happier. They smiled more and the spread of happiness was as infectious as influenza. I felt happy for the first time in many weeks. I spent many free hours either alone or with my nurse colleagues, lazing on the well-cultivated lawns or revising for my nursing studies. I was able to explore Yorkshire without any worry of the cold weather and I began to appreciate the peculiarities of Yorkshire life, the indigenous people as well as the immigrant minorities.

The ethnic diversity of Wakefield in the mid-1960s, as I perceived it, consisted mainly of Caucasian peoples, with flecks of other groups like Asians, West Indians and Africans. There were other minority Caucasian groups like the Polish and the Irish, and during my time in Wakefield one of my friends was another student nurse who was Polish. Her name was Jadwiga and her husband was also Polish. She told me that they had lived in Wakefield for many years, but Jadwiga still spoke English with a thick Polish accent. She reminded me of an army officer because she walked with an erect posture and with military precision in each quick footstep. Her black stockings had thick seams that ran down the back of her legs and her black highly polished shoes had thick heels of about five centimetres. The heels clunked heavily on the ground as she walked. Her nursing uniform was neat like that of any other student nurse at the time, but because of her bright red lipstick which coordinated with her hair colour, she stood out like a red flag. Her red lips became more noticeable when she blew smoke rings as she savoured the taste of her cigarette. She always smoked after the lunch break. Jadwiga spent countless hours trying to teach me basic Polish greetings, but many months passed before I could say *dzien dobry*, which means 'good morning'. Whenever I tried to repeat the greeting she collapsed in a heap of giggles. It was hilarious even to me, as I tried to speak Polish with my thick Bajan accent. We often talked about Poland and Barbados and I developed some knowledge about Poland and Polish culture. I was never brave enough to ask Jadwiga about her reason for coming to Britain, but I inferred from our talks that it was because of the Second World War and the hardship associated with the aftermath of war. Unfortunately I lost contact with her after leaving Wakefield, but I still remember Jadwiga's red lipstick, her red hair, her plumes of cigarette smoke and *dzien dobry*. Jadwiga was the only Pole I knew personally then, but over the years I have worked with other Poles in different professional capacities. I perceived them to be courteous, jovial and friendly, just like Jadwiga – but without the red lipstick.

I formed good relationships with several other student nurses in Wakefield. Some friendships were work-related, while others were in my main social circles. I often had tea with those friends and their families, and a Yorkshire 'tea' did not only mean the beverage, but was a grand affair with sandwiches, cakes, cream and lots of chatter and laughter. I relished these tea parties, especially during the summer months. My social friends outside the West Indian group were mainly white indigenous Yorkshire folk. At that time it was the exception rather than the rule to encounter a black person in Wakefield. We West Indian nurses were indeed happy when we discovered that there were other black student nurses in other neighbouring hospitals. We eventually developed connections with some of those nurses and were able to host joint parties. Although many of the party group were of African or West Indian origin, others were white or Asian. We were able to talk about our experiences as black student nurses in a 'white' country at these parties. We often used the party forum to console each other as we exchanged experiences of unpleasant situations, even though those situations were not as frequent as they could have been. Still, it was not unusual to hear about patients being verbally abusive. Sometimes patients became angry when black nurses approached them to deliver nursing care. I had one experience when a patient barked, 'Take your black hands off me!' I was mortified, but somehow had to maintain a professional approach. Fortunately a senior nurse, who was white, intervened to diffuse the potentially volatile situation. Over the years I became more adept at dealing with racism in nursing, and even though government legislation now protects carers and patients in the health professions, racism unfortunately still exists.

It was imperative that we received permission from the matron to hold parties. All parties ended at eleven o'clock at night and not a second earlier, not a second later. I was never able to make sense of the eleven o'clock deadline, but rules were set in stone and no one was exempt. A senior nurse whose designation was 'home sister' kept order in relation to behaviour and time whenever there was a party. Happily, she performed her duty with professionalism and equity.

The nurses from the neighbouring hospitals continued to network with us and other young black persons in the locality, so that eventually the group included an engineer and several students who were studying at local universities. The engineer had been living in Yorkshire for a few years and was able to help us to find our way around. He was called Bentfield and was one of the daddies of the group, although he was no older than the rest of us. I lost contact with most of the party group, including Bentfield, when I moved from Yorkshire to Nottingham in 1968, but several years later I re-established contact with several of them, Bentfield included. It was heartening to discover that nearly all of the party group were very successful, and one was rich enough to own a private jet in the West Indies. He had branched out from nursing to management and it had proved an excellent move. The social support network of the group was an element that helped me through those bleak early years in

Yorkshire. We often used West Indian anecdotes to minimise the stress of daily life. Humour was also a part of daily life in the hospital and was an antidote to situations that were potentially frustrating and provocative. Humorous situations were not exclusive to patients or nurses, but involved everyone who was part of the hospital daily buzz.

Communication breakdown between the 'foreign' staff and their colleagues, as well as between patients and the 'foreign' staff, was not unusual and was the source of many hilarious and embarrassing moments. During my early months in England I had to make a special effort to use the local vernacular, especially when I was communicating with patients, in order to avoid those potentially disastrous moments.

I remember one situation in which there was total communication breakdown between myself and a senior nurse, during my first six months in England. It still reduces me to laughter now. One day the senior nurse was explaining a nursing procedure to me in the treatment room. The door to the room was ajar and she said to me, 'Put t'wood in t'hole, luv.' I stared blankly at her. To me she was talking incomprehensible gibberish. As far as she was concerned, it was an everyday Yorkshire expression. The senior nurse stared at me with an equally blank expression for a few seconds, then realised that she should have communicated to me in 'English'. She tried again. 'Please close the door, love.' That was better!

I realised that using the word 'luv' or 'love' was a normal part of communication and was not said by Yorkshire people to be condescending or rude. The word 'love' eventually became part of my own vocabulary until I travelled to Nottingham to continue my nurse training.

I chose Nottingham entirely at random from several other training schools that advertised for student nurses who had a nursing qualification similar to the one that I possessed, the SEN (State Enrolled Nurse). I was ignorant of the geography and other important features of Nottingham and I knew no one there. It was either bravery or foolhardiness that motivated me to make such a risky choice – I'm not sure which – but I never regretted it. Nottingham is the city where I completed the nursing course to become a registered nurse and commenced midwifery training to become a registered midwife. I enjoyed living in Nottingham because, like Yorkshire, the pace of life was easy and I was cocooned in the security of the nurses' home. By then I was twenty years old and was beginning to appreciate the advantages of living and working in the safety of the hospital and the nurses' home.

My immediate perception of the two counties was that there was a significant difference in the vernacular. On my first day in Nottingham, I realised that I had to learn to speak like the Nottingham natives and dispense with the Yorkshire vernacular, because some of my Yorkshire expressions would doubtless 'raise eyebrows' in Nottingham. The need for the urgent change was most obvious on my first day when I hailed a taxi at the Nottingham railway station. The friendly taxi driver enquired about my origins and was interested to know where I had started my journey. When I told him that I had travelled from Yorkshire, he let out a mighty roar of laughter. The roar became spasmodic chuckles. During one of the pauses in the chain of chuckles he asked me if I had said 'Yarkshuh'. I stared at the back of his head as it jerked from one side to the other. I was in a state of disbelief and confusion, wondering what had caused the taxi driver to come so close to hysteria. He continued to chuckle to himself as he muttered, 'Yarkshuh, she said Yarkshuh...' By the time he deposited me at the reception of my new nurses' home, I was also chuckling. I was not sure if my amusement stemmed from embarrassment or bewilderment, but I vowed to take all precautions to sound 'less Yorkshire'.

Nottingham is a city in Nottinghamshire, a county in central England. It is famous for Sherwood Forest and the legend of Robin Hood. It lies about 30 miles (48 kilometres) from Yorkshire and about 107 miles (175 kilometres) from London. I enjoyed several visits to Sherwood Forest with some of the friends I made during my time there. One of my peers, whom I will refer to as Winnie, was a keen motor-scooter rider with a quest for adventure. I spent many hours as a pillion rider on her scooter as we toured Nottingham-shire. I was as adventurous as Winnie and loved to feel the wind on my back as we sped along the country lanes. She was very conscious about safety, though, and we always wore our crash helmets. She had lived in Sweden for a short time, even though she arrived there not knowing a word of Swedish. It was all part of her spirit of adventure. She managed to learn Swedish while she was there, and even tried to teach me when we were not studying nursing or looking for adventure in Nottinghamshire. I did not learn much, though, and Winnie soon married and moved away from Nottingham. I eventually also left to study for the second part of the midwifery course in Hertfordshire. Winnie and I corresponded for many years after our departure from Nottingham. During that time she and her husband became proud parents of several offspring. Eventually our correspondence ceased because of my several changes of location in England and their own relocation to a county in the west of England.

My move to Hertfordshire was a random selection, not unlike the route I took when I chose Nottingham. I enjoyed studying and working in Hertfordshire, partly because of its close proximity to London and partly because it was a suburban county. Hertford-shire is immediately north of Greater London. The most southern Hertfordshire town is about 10 miles (16.1 kilometres) from central London. I spent only a short time in Hertfordshire, however, because of my yearning to return to Barbados. In the following chapters I will share some of the memorable experiences I had in Hertfordshire and the other counties when I describe some of the intricacies of learning nursing and midwifery. The peculiarities of the various facets of nursing and midwifery which embraced different counties and countries became more meaningful to me as I moved from one county to another during those early years.

Studying and working in a variety of counties in

England made it easier for me to adjust and adapt to each of the local vernaculars and cultures as I travelled around. This in turn made it easier for me to interact effectively with a variety of patients and work colleagues. Understanding Cockney rhyming slang, however, was a surreal task. I learned that there was even variation in the Cockney expressions and that made it even more difficult for me to grasp the meanings of verbal exchanges with Cockneys when I first arrived in East London. After working in East London for many years, I have been able to make more sense of it, and I now understand terms like 'trouble and strife', which means 'wife', or 'brown bread', which means 'dead', or 'bin lids', which means 'kids' or 'children'.

Many years ago, a Cockney woman called Gwen told me that a true Cockney is a person who was born within the sound of the Bow Bells of St Mary-le-Bow Church in Cheapside, London. However, it appears that the term Cockney is now loosely applied to people who might have been born outside the St Mary-le-Bow Church area, as long as they have a Cockney accent or a Cockney heritage. The Cockney accent is not heard in central London today as much as it was earlier. It is now heard in the outer London boroughs, however, as well as the London suburbs and all across south-east England. This variation in the distribution of the accent is due to the migration of Cockneys to these areas over the years.

Although my work colleagues included people from all over Britain as well as people from other countries in the world during my years in the caring professions, I am still fascinated by the Yorkshire accent when I compare it with the several accents to which I was exposed after my arrival in England. I am still able to translate some of the Yorkshire expressions when I hear them and often muse on the occasions when *faux pas* were the order of my early days in Wakefield. I always remember Wakefield with a touch of fondness, even though I bear the scars of some painful experiences. It was there that I had my initiation into the nursing profession. This initiation was only a glimpse of what was to become a tortuous course of peaks and troughs over decades of both lamentation and celebration.

Learning Nursing

The official commencement of the nursing course
was July 1966. The hospital authorities accepted the
Bajan trainee nurses two weeks in advance of the
official start date in order to give us time to orientate
to our new surroundings. We arrived in Wakefield on
a Friday afternoon and spent the weekend recovering
from the transatlantic journey and the remnant jetlag.
The tutor Miss Amy (not her real name) made
provision for us to receive the appropriate care over
the weekend in order that we would be refreshed
and ready for the real business of nursing by
Monday.

On my first Monday in England the tutor
accompanied me and the other new Bajans on a tour
of the hospital. I was bewildered by the long
corridors and the anxiety etched on the faces of the
patients, some with very pale, gaunt faces and sad
eyes, others with brighter eyes who managed to
smile at us. I had never been so close to a hospital
ward before, even though I had attended the
Casualty department in Barbados on several
occasions. I had never seen a bedpan before and I
was ignorant of the fact that men also used bedpans:
I had the notion that women used bedpans and men

used bottles for excretion purposes. It was indeed a shock for me when Miss Amy discovered my ignorance and spent a considerable length of time trying to educate me on the rudiments of excretion receptacles. By the end of the tour my head was spinning with the volume of information the tutor had given us, and I was concerned about how I was going to absorb all the nursing information when the course finally commenced.

The tutor explained that we would have to spend the first two weeks in the hospital to get used to the environment and gain an insight into the complexities of caring for sick people. The working day started at eight o'clock in the morning and finished at five o'clock in the evening, with scheduled breaks in the mid-morning and the afternoon, and I did find the days long, monotonous and tedious. I had only just left school and had never undertaken any compulsory work before, although I had assisted an older friend with needlework. She worked at home for a company and had tight deadlines to submit the finished products and often engaged my older sister and me when her schedule was critical and she still had many pieces of work to complete. The money I received from her was the main source of my pocket money and I used the meagre earnings to buy items that were essential to teenage existence. That was a relief for me and my parents because they did not have to worry about stretching their limited resources to meet my need for pocket money. Handcraft work is no comparison to sustained compulsory work, however, and so I was nearly collapsing by the end of each day during my early weeks in Yorkshire. I eagerly looked forward to resting at the end of the day and especially at the weekend.

My first mentor was the ward orderly (I will call her Mary), who seemed to be busy throughout each hour that she was on duty. Mary was a married woman of average height and size who might have been about thirty-four years old. She had piercing blue eyes and very blonde, almost white hair that she wore in a short neat style. Her skin was very pale compared to the tanned skin of the white people I was used to seeing in Barbados. She wore pale lipstick which exaggerated the pallor of her face, and at our first meeting I wondered if Mary was ill, although I soon reasoned that she would not have been on the ward working if she was ill. She spoke quietly, but with a measure of authority, and expected me to be as busy as she was. It was very difficult for me to work at her pace because the Bajan pace of life to which I was accustomed was like a crawl in the park compared with the sprint that I had to maintain to keep up with Mary. I was Mary's shadow during my first two weeks on the ward and I followed her around like a young puppy that had just been plucked from a litter of seven.

Mary showed me how to scrub the metal bedpans, bottles, sputum mugs and tooth mugs, and the smells from the carbolic and other disinfectants that we used always permeated the sluice room. The smell clung to my uniform like a strong perfume and it was very difficult to get rid of it when I had completed my duties. Mary also taught me how to change flower vases and arrange new flowers when the patients' relatives brought in their daily supply of roses, carnations, daffodils and other beautiful flowers. The fruit bowls had to be arranged in a decorative fashion after the fruit had been washed in the metal kitchen sink. Individual patient lockers and bed tables were washed daily with disinfectant, and bed-making was an art of arranging crisp white sheets and pillowcases with neat, precisely creased ends – and all in time for the matron's ward round.

Many of the skills that I acquired during those days are still fresh in my mind, but the approach to the practice of some of those skills has changed considerably in the twenty-first century. It appears that nursing priorities in caring for patients have been modified markedly. It is debatable whether or not the changed priorities have enhanced patient care and patient recovery outcomes. One of the obvious changes is the absence of the matron's ward round. This was designed to give the matron the opportunity to obtain a summary of how the patient population was faring and take appropriate action to resolve any issues that could undermine patient recovery. The matron's ward round was a like a royal visit, although it was in reality a kind of military procession that occurred at any time from mid-morning onwards. The senior nurse who was in charge of the ward at that time had to introduce each patient to the matron, noting briefly the patient's name, diagnosis and treatment. It was a stressful time for all the nurses who were present on duty, and student nurses like myself sought refuge in the sluice room until the 'storm' had passed, unless we were identified specifically to accompany the senior nurse on the matron's round. The round seemed like an eternity, especially for petrified students, because the wards were Victorian arrangements with about twenty-eight patients, fourteen on each side of the ward. There was an air of calm after the matron had left the ward and the sluice room refugees cautiously emerged from several nooks and crannies, having confirmed that the coast was clear.

Even the ward orderlies were *au fait* with the etiquette that surrounded the matron's ward round and, like Mary, they continued quietly with their duties during the procession. Ward orderlies complemented the workforce and were invaluable in maintaining a good ward environment. They were the equivalent of today's health care assistants, but had a wider remit: they were like a band of warriors who silently fought against grease, grime and germs. I will never know if ward orderlies had any idea of their value in scientific terms, in the prevention of infection and the ultimate well-being of themselves, the staff and the patients, but I became acutely aware that a good clean working environment was critical both to the practical experiences of the student nurses and the recovery of the patients. I felt that Mary was successful in providing me with adequate orientation, because when I started the formal nursing studies, I was able to recognise some of the basic nursing care skills I had already seen in the theory of nursing care that the tutor presented to the class.

One basic but important skill that I acquired from Mary was how to present a meal to anyone, especially a sick person. I still apply the same technique when I entertain friends and family, because when a meal is presented in an attractive way, it stimulates the taste buds and the appetite in a way that enhances enjoyment of the food. I learned that when a meal is served, there should be no gravy spills on the edges of the plate, no splashes on the side of the dessert bowl; the cutlery should be clean, wrapped in a clean serviette and placed on the right side of the plate. When the recipient of the meal is a patient confined to bed, the bed table should be drawn up to a position where the patient can have easy access to the food. When I was learning nursing, it was the responsibility of each nurse who was present to ensure that each patient received some form of nourishment at each meal time. The ward sister or senior staff nurse usually did an after-meal inventory to confirm that no patient was left unfed.

I become sad when I hear of situations in the twenty-first century where the relatives of hospital in-patients have made complaints to the hospital managers or to the media that patients have not eaten their meals or have not been fed. There has even been media reporting of malnutrition amongst hospital patients. This should not be happening in this advanced technological era. Several reasons for this problem have been alluded to, but a solution must be found to ensure that patients leave hospital in a better condition than when they were admitted! Food was everybody's business during my early years in nursing and nurses were the main reference point in patient nourishment.

It was also deemed important that the nurses themselves should be well fed and nourished. The rationale for the provision of meals for nurses during working hours was that a nurse who was adequately nourished would be a more productive worker who in turn would provide better patient care. Today nurses do not enjoy the same nutritional concessions that I enjoyed, as they have to pay for their meals during their working hours. There is debate about whether or not some nurses now enjoy a good nutritional status and about how their nutritional status could impact on the quality of patient care. There is a Bajan saying, 'A hungry man is an angry man.' There may be some truth in this adage that could be applied to nurses, nutrition and patient care today.

Meal times for nurses during my training were really semi-formal occasions. Batches of nurses filed into the dining room with military precision for their meal break, and dinner was the highlight of the day. The junior nurses included auxiliary nurses, student nurses, enrolled nurses and staff nurses. The senior nurses included the senior staff nurses, junior sisters, senior sisters, deputy matron and the matron, in that order. The nurses ranking from auxiliary nurse, student nurse to sister were usually seated first.

The matron or her deputy entered the room to conduct the 'procedure' and immediately all nurses stood up as a mark of respect and awaited the signal to sit, following the grace of thanksgiving for the meal. Meals were in three courses and the senior nurses received their courses first, from soup to pudding (or 'sweet' as it was usually referred to in Yorkshire). Student nurses and auxiliary nurses, who were at the bottom of the hierarchy, received their courses last. The matron or her deputy always waited for the signal from the waitresses that everyone had finished the meal.

The waitresses were neatly turned out in well-ironed uniforms, white, crisply starched aprons, frilly white starched caps and gleaming polished shoes. They glided from table to table in an orderly, almost robotic fashion as they served each course. As if by instinct, the empty plates were removed in a similar fashion as each course followed. Once the matron confirmed with the waitresses that the meal was over, she stood up. This was an automatic signal to the other diners that they should follow suit. It was the unspoken duty of the junior nurse who was nearest to the exit door to open the door for the matron as she was leaving the room. The other diners continued the exodus in single file, ending with the exit of the junior nurses. This was the daily routine, which remained unvaried even on special occasions like Christmas, when the only significant difference was the festive trimmings with the Christmas pudding.

I enjoyed the Yorkshire cuisine and especially relished the summer new potatoes, fresh sliced meats like ham, mountains of salad with fresh spring onions and lashings of salad cream, washed down with water and chased with a hot dessert. The chef was a marvellous former army man who had a broad, cheerful smile. His grin exposed a flashing gold incisor like a thin beam of light coming from a slit in a set of drawn curtains. He was a gourmet with a sixth sense for foods of the world. He always ensured that the immigrant nurses, including me, received some element in their evening meal that reflected the tropics.

Good nourishment was essential, considering that the working week was in excess of forty hours, inclusive of study days in the nursing school. There were established days off, of course, and annual leave provided welcome relief from the intensity of caring and studying. Learning nursing was no pleasure cruise!

The first formal weeks of the nursing course were orientation or introductory weeks. During the introductory period we were taken on visits to places like the local sewage works, the local water treatment plant and other such facilities. I was puzzled at first about the rationale behind such seemingly unrelated places, but realised very soon that the sewage plant must deal effectively with waste matter in order to prevent and contain the spread of diseases. Safe drinking water was necessary to keep the population hydrated as well as to prevent the spread of infection through cleansing. The relevance of the other facilities eventually became clearer as I continued my nursing studies.

My year group of 1966 in Wakefield was comprised of twelve mainly single females with an age range of eighteen to the mid-thirties. There were no male students in my cohort. My good friend Jadwiga was one of the oldest members of the group and I was one of the youngest. Study days involved learning anatomy and the physiology of the body systems and receiving practical demonstrations in the clinical learning room on various aspects of patient care. Simulated patient care is no substitute for real care, as I discovered when I gave my first intramuscular injection. I had been participating in nursing care for a few months and had practised administering an intramuscular injection on several occasions in the clinical classroom, using an orange to simulate the gluteal muscle – but fear, anxiety and shaking hands were the things that I remember about that first real injection.

There is a standard procedure for administering any form of medication to a patient and I could recite the procedure faultlessly: preparing and checking (with a senior nurse) of the medication as prescribed by the doctor, identifying of the correct patient, explaining what is about to happen, obtaining the patient's permission to administer the medicine, ensuring patient privacy, administering the medicine, leaving the patient in a comfortable state and recording the medication on the patient's documents.

In theory this was a straightforward procedure, but in practice it was a giant step for me, a mere teenager who was about to perform an adult procedure. The senior nurse who was my mentor on that occasion accompanied me to the patient's bed and explained that I, the student nurse, would be administering the injection if the patient had no objection. The patient was a middle-aged woman who was very obliging as she was used to the procedure after her long stay in hospital; she was being treated for tuberculosis. An intramuscular injection is usually administered in the upper outer aspect of the gluteal or buttocks muscle in order to avoid injecting the medication into the sciatic nerve which runs down the back of the leg. This nerve branches from the spinal cord and injecting medication into it could cause paralysis.

The senior nurse assisted me to put the patient on her side, exposing only the area that was required for the injection. The only things in my focus at that time were a broad expanse of human tissue and my own shaking hands. I managed to clean the injection site with a swab soaked in surgical spirit. I lifted the syringe that was filled with the medication from the kidney-shaped container, raised it to a vertical position and made sure that there was no air in the syringe; air in the syringe could cause problems in the patient, especially if the injection was given by the intravenous route. The voice of the senior nurse was light years away from my consciousness as she made conversation with the patient while keeping her eyes fixed on me. Somehow I managed to insert the needle into the ample muscle. I withdrew the plunger slightly to confirm that there was no trace of blood in the syringe. Any trace of blood would indicate that I had punctured a blood vessel. In that situation I would need to remove the needle from the site and repeat the insertion in another site, but still in the upper outer quadrant of the gluteal muscle. Fortunately, I had inserted the needle into the muscle and I was able to slowly inject the medication as the senior nurse discreetly helped to steady my hand. It was with great relief that I withdrew the needle and kept pressure on the injection site with a cotton swab until there was no sign of blood loss. I thanked the patient for her help, and the senior nurse and I left her in a comfortable position. We completed the patient records and then proceeded to the treatment room that was located at the end of the ward.

I needed time to control my shaking hands and recover from the experience. I was relieved that I had not fainted from the panic I had experienced during the procedure, and the senior nurse was also relieved that I had scaled the first injection hurdle. I became more confident as I continued to administer injections to a variety of patients, but I will always remember the kind woman who consented to a young novice practising on her gluteal muscle. She was one of several patients who presented with a variety of medical conditions during the time of my practical experience on the ward.

I have a vivid memory of some of the more complicated medical conditions that I encountered during my early nursing experiences. Adult respiratory infections like bronchitis and tuberculosis and childhood infections like whooping cough (pertussis) are some of them.

The most disturbing of these for me as a young inexperienced student nurse was whooping cough in children. Childhood immunisation for whooping cough was introduced in the 1950s. Despite this preventative approach to the disease, the incidence of whooping cough in children was still significant in the 1960s. The winter months often increased the potential for individuals to contract the illness and on some occasions I was involved with the care of several children who were admitted to hospital.

Pertussis or whooping cough is a bacterial infection of the respiratory tract by the organism *bordetella pertussis*. It is spread from one person to another by droplet infection; that is, through body functions like coughing and sneezing. Whooping cough may begin as an ordinary cold in a child, but within one or two weeks whooping cough could be diagnosed because of the sign of the peculiar cough that produces a 'whooping' sound. A typical coughing attack consists of a deep intake of air by the child. This intake of air is followed by a rapid series of explosive coughs when the child breathes out. The tongue protrudes and the face and lips become blue (cyanosed). The attack may end with another intake of air through a partially closed glottis. The glottis is the space between the vocal cords, and the vocal cords are located in the larynx (voice box). The glottis is the narrowest part of the upper respiratory passage and when a person swallows it is covered by a fold of tissue called the epiglottis. The epiglottis prevents any material from being inhaled into the air passage. The characteristic whooping sound that may be present in the child with whooping cough is caused by an intake of air through a partially closed glottis. The episode of paroxysms ends with the child vomiting and finally becoming prostrate with exhaustion.

I was petrified when I witnessed a child of about three years who was diagnosed with whooping cough having an attack of paroxysms. I was convinced that the child was on the verge of death during the episode, especially when she became blue in the face. An experienced nurse was present during the attack and reassured me that the child was not dying. She was correct in her assessment and the child recovered within a short space of time as she settled back onto her pillow completely exhausted. In order to prevent the spread of diseases like whooping cough, nurses routinely used masks and gowns and observed rigorous washing of their hands on entry to each cubicle and before leaving the cubicle. They also observed a specific technique to put gowns and gloves on and leave the cubicle without touching any objects, including the door.

Parents were not as involved with the care of their children then as they are today and were only able to see their children through the clear glass that separated each cubicle from the main corridor in the ward. The nurses were the surrogate parents who had to meet the physical and psychological needs of the children during the long periods of hospitalisation. When parents visited, the nurses and doctors communicated the progress of their children to them. Unfortunately, whooping episodes may last for about three months and serious complications including acute bronchitis, broncho-pneumonia and even death are associated with this disease. The children for whom I cared all made a full recovery after receiving intensive (barrier) nursing and medical care over many weeks. There is empirical evidence to support the recommendation that immunisation to prevent the suffering and distress of the type I observed is efficacious. The old adage, 'Prevention is better than cure', applies.

Another disease that requires patience, endurance and empathy over protracted periods of care is tuberculosis (TB). I nursed several patients with the condition during those early years. TB is a contagious bacterial disease; it is acquired by inhaling the tuberculosis bacilli from the spray that is emitted from individuals who are already infected with the disease when they cough or sneeze. It may also be acquired by ingesting cow's milk that is infected with the organism. The initial signs of TB infection are a cough, weight loss, fatigue and sweating at night. The disease is confirmed with the aid of a chest x-ray, microscopic sputum analysis and the Mantoux test. The condition requires prompt and rigorous treatment because it has the potential to spread via the bloodstream throughout the entire body. This can destroy body tissues and may prove fatal for the individual.

Treatment is a combination of medical, nutritional, social and psychological care over a long period of time. Rigorous monitoring of the patient's medication and progress is important to ensure that the medication is efficacious. Some of the drugs that may be used to treat TB could become toxic to the body and could affect the nervous system. The treatment could be prolonged over a few months or even years.

It was rewarding to see positive results of the

treatment for TB. I remember vividly one patient who was successfully treated. I shall refer to him as Ed. When I first met Ed, he was a picture of sadness. Ed was a coal miner who had seen his doctor because of a persistent cough. Investigations confirmed that he had contracted TB and he was admitted to hospital for treatment. Ed had sad eyes which sank into hollow eye sockets. He was pale and thin, with a haunted look. He appeared to be a cheerful person in normal life, but his condition only allowed him the painful effort of giving fleeting smiles in a sagging face. There were other male patients in the ward and over the weeks Ed's demeanour changed as he bonded with others who were also receiving treatment for TB. Ed's treatment was a regimen of anti-TB drugs, effective nursing care, good nutrition and regular monitoring by the physicians. He passed the time telling and listening to jokes (some fit for all ears, others reserved only for the brave), playing games like cards and sitting out in the sunshine when the weather permitted. Like the other patients, Ed loathed the winter months because activities were of necessity confined to the ward. Sleeping was the main pastime then. Still, sleep is essential to rest the body, allowing healing of the stressed body systems.

After what seemed like an eternity, Ed was discharged from the hospital with instructions to continue his care as an outpatient. His gaunt, haunted expression had disappeared, his blue eyes were dancing and his cheeks were plump. His trousers were fitting snugly around his waist and were no longer a pair of baggy overalls. Ed was a prime example of the typical patient who was treated successfully for TB. The success was a testament of his endurance as well as that of his family and the dedication and persistence of those who cared for him.

Patients like Ed who were infected with TB usually looked like they had been exposed to the ravages of a severe famine when they first arrived at the hospital, but when the treatment was successful they were discharged looking as though they had feasted at sumptuous banquets for many seasons. There were many success stories like Ed's and I felt proud to be part of the good outcomes. I was very relieved that I did not witness any deaths that resulted from TB and I am not aware of any deaths that occurred during my nurse training.

TB is still problematic in the twenty-first century and scientists are concerned about the possibility of the organism that causes the disease becoming resistant to some of the drugs that are used to treat the condition. It is debatable whether or not the stigma that was synonymous with TB during my early years in nursing still exists. Perhaps the propagation of knowledge about the disease and the availability and effectiveness of treatment have reduced the level of anxiety in people regarding TB.

Caring for patients with infectious diseases was both challenging and rewarding, and was an opportunity to search for more information about the conditions in order to improve my nursing care of those patients. The practice of nursing demanded a continuous downloading of theoretical knowledge.

The nursing school and the complement of tutors were responsible for helping students to make sense of the theoretical knowledge and apply that knowledge to the practical care of patients. They fed us more and more knowledge as the months passed and on some occasions I even felt good about my own knowledge base! I was the epitome of modesty, however, so I never implied that I knew much. I was being very cautious.

The senior tutor Miss Amy was responsible for the overall education and pastoral care of the students, especially the 'overseas nurses'. She was the link between the wards and the students and monitored the progress of the students with the help of the ward nurses and her clinical classroom tutors and assistants.

Miss Amy was a pleasant, friendly, critically aware woman in her early forties. She was single, like most senior nurses in those days, but had a very motherly approach to the welfare of 'her' nurses. She was an effective role model who inspired confidence in the students and encouraged them to progress in the nursing profession. I mention this outstanding quality because her advice to me personally was a catalyst for my striving to excel in nursing. When I was selected to study nursing in England, I was naive about the hierarchy that existed in the nursing profession. I was of the belief that there was just one category of trained nurse. However, when I had undergone about six months of training, I discovered that there were two categories of qualified nurse, namely the SRN (State Registered Nurse) and the SEN

(State Enrolled Nurse). The difference between the two categories was that the SEN was a practical nurse qualification. The course for the SEN lasted two years. Qualification was based on passing a practical and theoretical examination. The SRN was a more advanced qualification with the potential for the holder to progress in the profession. The course for the SRN lasted three years and qualification was based on passing a practical and theoretical examination at a more advanced level. The course on which I was enrolled was for the SEN qualification, and offered little or no prospects of advancement in the profession.

I was fortunate to have been educated at high school level and possessed the GCE (General Certificate of Education). On that basis I was accepted on a course to train for a further two years to obtain the SRN qualification in another establishment. I successfully passed the theoretical and practical examinations at the end of the two years. I was extremely proud of my achievement when I was awarded the SRN, even though I had to study for four years, rather than the usual three, to obtain the qualification. I was able to pursue other advanced courses as a result of possessing the SRN qualification and was rewarded with several other vocational professional and academic qualifications over the remainder of my career. I felt justified for being proactive in those early years in pursuing the details of the SRN course and eventually securing such an important career springboard.

In addition to learning nursing during my early

years in England, I was able to travel to other countries in the West Indies, United Kingdom, Europe and Africa. I was able to make the distinction between England as a separate country and England as part of the United Kingdom or Great Britain – which I discovered was made up of England, Scotland, Wales and Northern Ireland. Prior to this discovery, I was aware only of England, which was described by most Bajans as the 'mother country', and although I had heard of Scotland, Ireland and Wales, I conceptualised the three countries as being entirely separate from England.

During my travels to and through countries like France, Germany, Spain and Africa, I was able to learn about the languages and cultures of different peoples. I used this knowledge to enhance my care of patients other than English or British patients, whenever the opportunity arose. As a result of my own experiences, I have always entertained the idea that nursing knowledge in isolation, without additional knowledge of different people groups and cultures, is like salad without the dressing or roast beef without the Yorkshire pudding. One discipline in the caring professions that emphasises the significance of understanding different people and cultures is midwifery. I made that discovery when I trained to be a midwife.

Learning Midwifery

Knowledge of the peculiarities of different peoples and cultures is absolutely essential when caring for women during birth experiences. There is usually a sustained period of personal contact between the carers, the woman and her partner during the entire childbearing cycle, more than in any other caring situation.

It was ironic that, for the second time in my life, I made a choice of career pathway through my own observations of the professional behaviours and attitudes of expert practitioners. My first career choice was made after observing nurses practising in the Casualty department in Barbados during my child-hood. During my practice as a registered nurse following qualification, I frequently socialised with midwives from the maternity department in the general hospital where I worked. We often exchanged ideas about our specific practices and I realised that there was something about midwifery that was markedly different from nursing. Nursing was involved with assisting ill individuals to get better, and it was always rewarding to save the lives of people who in some instances were near death when they were admitted to the hospital. Midwifery, on the other hand, was involved with assisting and supporting prospective parents through a normal biological process – or, in simple terms, helping 'Mother Nature'. After practising as a nurse for about a year, I was persuaded to transfer the skills and attitudes that I had developed to learning midwifery. Subsequently, midwifery became my first love in the caring professions and I continued in that speciality for the rest of my active career, both as a practitioner and as an educator.

Midwifery is unlike any other discipline in the caring professions and events surrounding the birth process appear to leave a lasting mental print on the parents as well as the carers, even when an event is uncomplicated. When the process is fraught with complications, it appears that the mental print is more acute and sustained especially in the individual woman, but also in her partner and her carers.

The aim of care in any birth event is to have an uncomplicated birth with a live and healthy mother and baby at the end of it. However, when eventualities arise, the midwife has the expertise to recognise when the assistance of an obstetrician is imperative, according to specific rules that govern the practice of midwifery. The obstetrician would in turn seek the assistance of other specialists like the physician, the surgeon and the anaesthetist if and when the problem warrants their particular expertise.

British midwifery in the twenty-first century is unlike midwifery in the 1960s. A dynamic process of change has been the main reason for the present status of midwifery as a much specialised, research-based profession, with midwives being taught in institutions of higher education. As a result of this evolving trend, there are now professors of midwifery and some midwives also hold doctorate degrees.

Another major change in British midwifery is the presence of men in midwifery care. The male midwife now plays a significant role in childbearing, not unlike that of the traditional female midwife. The significant difference between the male and female roles is that male midwives have to be more acutely aware of the safeguards required when performing invasive midwifery procedures that require sensitivity and privacy. Some women and their partners may object to the provision of midwifery care by a male midwife because of preference, culture or religion. The male midwife as a practitioner is acutely aware of this type of potential eventuality and would adapt to the situation and take appropriate action.

The presence of men in midwifery was surrounded by taboo even in the sixteenth century, when doctors attempted to get involved with birthing. The male midwife of the sixteenth century was the forerunner of the obstetrician and had to struggle for many years to be included in a practice that was perceived to be solely the domain of women.

In more modern times, the male midwife emerged from a campaign by male nurses that followed the implementation of the Sex Discrimination Act (1976) in Britain. The first Midwives Act (1902) was concerned with the training and practice of female midwives in order to protect the public. Prior to this act, midwifery care was performed by women who in many instances were ignorant of the basic facts of anatomy and obstetrics. Later on, the Midwives Act (1952) did not include men practising midwifery.

The Sex Discrimination Act (1976) did not alter the status quo, because midwifery at that time was exempt from the Sex Discrimination Act. The British government was subsequently pressured into giving consideration to the voice of the men who wanted to train to be midwives. Two experimental training schemes were sanctioned to train men as midwives. One scheme was facilitated in England and the other in Scotland. The first men entered midwifery training in 1977. The results of the experiments supported the notion that men could function effectively in midwifery and the exclusion of men from the practice was removed in 1983. British men still make up only a small percentage of midwives, accounting for about 0.2 per cent of midwives in Britain today. More than 150 British men have trained as midwives, but less than 100 of these practise midwifery in the twenty-first century. Yet some of the men have been elevated to the positions of senior managers and lecturers during the years that they have been active in midwifery.

Midwifery is perceived by many people as another discipline in nursing: a nurse should be able to care for sick people to help them get better as well as able to deliver babies when a pregnancy reaches the due date. In Britain, however, the art of midwifery is exclusive of nursing *per se* and the British midwife will always emphasise the uniqueness of the art –

whereas in some countries midwifery is part of the role of the obstetric nurse and the onus of the birth process is laid on the obstetrician. Many trained midwives in Britain are also qualified nurses, but in recent years many midwives have followed a single training pathway to become qualified. The single pathway was previously a two-year programme but has now been extended to three years. Still, during the three-year programme, the students receive instructions in medical nursing and other crucial and relevant aspects of nursing. Nursing knowledge is applied to midwifery when medical conditions develop during a pregnancy. Qualified nurses, on the other hand, follow an eighteen-month midwifery programme. Yet midwifery programmes are all now facilitated at diploma or undergraduate level.

Medical conditions in a pregnant woman tend to behave in peculiar ways and unless the midwife is critically aware of these peculiarities, he or she could contribute to morbidity and mortality in the mother and baby. The programmes of study are therefore designed to cater for this and other related knowledge bases. A competent midwife can only provide quality care for women and their partners if he or she has the knowledge, skills and attitude that would inspire confidence. These traits or qualities are acquired through an intensive programme of theory and practice, including a period of practice with mentor support, after passing the appropriate assessments during and at the end of the programme.

A British midwife by virtue of his or her training is able to care for a pregnant woman throughout the entire process on his or her own responsibility, although it is necessary to engage the provision of a medical practitioner to cater for potential problems that may occur at any stage of the process. A few midwives practise independently, but their practice is controlled by the same authorities that govern midwifery as a whole.

Midwifery is a complex discipline that involves caring for both women and babies. The care of the woman commences even before conception occurs. This care is important to prepare the woman and her partner for the demands of pregnancy, birth and the period after the birth. The aim of preconception care is to stabilise the physical well-being of the woman and her partner and also to promote their psychological well-being. This preparation also identifies baseline measurements, especially for the woman, so that during the childbearing process the woman's carers are able to recognise the early signs of potential complications so that appropriate responses can be initiated.

The client-centred care continues throughout the pregnancy, birth and postnatal periods through a process of monitoring, recording, educating and advising the mothers. The partners are included in the process because there is evidence to suggest that an informed partner would be more alert to the needs of the woman and therefore more able to support her throughout the entire childbearing process.

When I started training to be a midwife, the profession was dominated by females. Males who were involved in childbearing were medical personnel like obstetricians. The training programme was a two-part course, each part lasting for six months. The first part involved intensive theory and practice of midwifery and understanding the role of related services. At the end of the course, the student sat a theory and practice examination. In order to qualify for the certificate, the candidate had to pass both parts. The certificate did not give the student licence to work as a midwife: it was the entry requirement to continue with the second part of the midwifery training.

Part two of the course focused on consolidating the theory and practice of part one, while also looking at the knowledge base in the context of care in a community setting and dealing with situations that could complicate childbearing. Emphasis was placed on the significance of the National Health Service provisions through dentists, opticians, pharmacists, social workers, health visitors, GPs (general medical practitioners) and other key health care providers. The role of religious leaders was also covered. It was not unusual for religious leaders to visit the parents and the newborn baby at home or in hospital, to say prayers and to welcome the baby.

Legislation was highlighted during each part of the midwifery course. Students were expected to be versed in general legislation and its impact on midwifery, as well as legislation specific to the training and practice of midwifery, including birth registration and the administration of medicines.

At the end of the second part of training, the student was examined in the relevant theory and practice and, again, passing both parts of the examination was imperative.

A mandatory fee had to be paid to the CMB (Central Midwives Board) after passing both parts of the course, in order that the qualified midwife could be recognised as registered and able to practise midwifery. There was a separate CMB for England and Wales, Scotland, and Northern Ireland that controlled the training, examination and practice of midwives in each country, but the Boards collaborated in the discharge of their responsibilities to protect the public through the provision of competent midwives who were fit for practice.

In 1979 the CMBs along with the General Nursing Councils for England and Wales, Scotland and Northern Ireland were amalgamated under a new statutory framework for the regulation of nurses, midwives and health visitors in Britain. The UKCC (United Kingdom Central Council) was created to maintain a register of qualified nurses, health visitors and midwives and to set standards for education, practice and conduct. The UKCC established four National Boards to discharge the Council's duties. A Parliamentary Order in 2001 changed the UKCC to the NMC (Nursing and Midwifery Council), which was put into effect in 2002.

Before the inception of the UKCC, qualified nurses, midwives and health visitors paid a registration fee after qualification to be placed on an appropriate register and the fee was designed to cover the practice of the individual for life. After 1992, the UKCC levied three-yearly periodic registration fees on all qualified nurses, midwives and health visitors. The name of the practitioner could be removed from the register if the fees were not paid.

There is a statutory requirement of midwives to demonstrate that they have undertaken continued professional refreshment or development. Evidence of refreshment is monitored both by the local Supervisor of Midwives and the NMC, and failure to comply could affect registration to practise as a midwife. Nurses also have to demonstrate continued professional refreshment, but they are not as fettered by statute as the midwives. However, they have to demonstrate that they have had refreshment at each periodic renewal of their registration to practise as nurses.

Training to be a midwife in the 1970s was more demanding than training to be a nurse. I entered training with a cohort of qualified nurses. Most of them had one year or more of practice following qualification as nurses and some of the cohort had been practising at ward manager level.

During the first week of training, I realised that a different coping strategy was required to survive the midwifery course. I was demoralised when I discovered that we would have to revisit basic anatomy and physiology. The tutor reminded us that it was her duty to ensure that we knew every detail of anatomy, especially anatomy related to child-bearing. Later, I saw the relevance of such detailed knowledge to midwifery practice. Basic anatomy and physiology related to childbearing was difficult. I was surprised to learn, for example, that there was some relevance of geometry to the angles of the female pelvis; that when a woman is standing in the upright position, her pelvis is not at right angles to the spine and the inlet of the pelvis slopes at an angle of about 60°. Any geometric deviations from the normal pelvic measurements could adversely influence the outcome of the birth process. It was also interesting to be able to appreciate the significance of genetic influences on some of the peculiarities of the female pelvis. Knowledge of the peculiarities was critical during birth experiences. A midwife who was ignorant of such facts could erroneously diagnose problems in the labour process when in reality the genetic peculiarity in a particular woman would equate with normal progress in her situation.

I spent countless hours reciting every detail of an anatomical model of the female pelvis. This was compounded by also trying to grasp the details of an anatomical model of the foetal (unborn baby's) skull. I discovered that the skull in the foetus and newborn baby is a maze of spaces and soft bones. The midwifery course demanded that I knew every minute detail of that maze, as well as every curve and straight of the female pelvis. Periods of frustration were followed by periods of sheer relief when I identified the correct measurements.

On many occasions frustration led to tears from me as well as most of the others in the cohort. I felt humiliated because, as a registered nurse, I did not perceive myself as an idiot, yet in terms of midwifery anatomy, I was a complete novice. Some of the others in the cohort who were mothers and spouses were not exempt from the humiliation. We cried alone, with each other and for each other, and licked our wounded egos together – but we never expressed such emotion in the presence of the patients and their relatives. We supported each other continuously and whenever we erred in our recall of the level of knowledge that the course demanded of us, we spent time together rehearsing and reciting the items that were alien to us. It was not unusual for student midwives to attempt to discontinue the training (and my cohort was no exception), but during our ego repair sessions we consoled and persuaded each other to continue in the course. We succeeded because we supported each other.

Throughout the course, students were always mentored by experienced midwives. Initially, the student observed the midwives as they practised, then the student practised the same procedures with guidance. Eventually the student practised with supervision and the midwives adjusted the level of supervision according to the progress and development of the student. Newly qualified midwives were also supported by more experienced midwives in the early period following qualification. The midwife who supported me following my qualification was a fount of knowledge and skills. She did not entertain half measures in any aspect of practice, humanity or professionalism.

I was mesmerised when I witnessed the first delivery of a baby, because instead of delivering one baby as expected, the midwife was thrown into overdrive when she realised that there was a second baby. It was a case of undiagnosed twins! The midwife was supervising a medical student who was delivering her first baby – medical students also have to gain experience in midwifery when they are training to be doctors. The midwife had safely guided the medical student through the delivery of the baby and we were waiting for delivery of the placenta, or afterbirth. There is usually a time gap between the birth of the baby and the delivery of the placenta, and the midwife must be vigilant but not hasty in order to avoid complications like haemorrhage in the mother.

I had never seen a human placenta, so I was confused when the midwife, with bulging eyes and hands hovering in readiness to intervene, asked the medical student to rupture the membranes. The medical student was as much a novice as I was and froze in panic, so the midwife quickly ruptured the bulging membranes herself – and another baby followed the swift flow of liquor. The medical student and I needed some time to overcome the shock of the experience, and the parents needed time to adjust to having twins, as they were prepared for one baby. Their emotions were an understandable mixture of pleasure and anxiety, but during the postnatal period they were given the necessary support and advice in order for them to provide optimum care for the twins. The midwife carried on with her duties as though an emergency had never occurred. Later she explained to me that the second baby was at risk of hypoxia, a shortage of oxygen. There was a possibility that once the first baby was delivered, the placenta would start to separate from its attachment to the mother's uterus or womb. Shortage of oxygen could lead to injury to the baby's brain, and even death. She emphasised that speed balanced with safety is the essence of the delivery of the second baby during a twin birth.

Technology in midwifery care has reduced the incidence of undiagnosed twins, but at that time such technology was a mere embryonic innovation. Midwives and obstetricians depended mainly on their own visual and tactile clinical observations and had an endless reserve of expertise that they applied to making diagnoses. Technology has made it possible today to diagnose even the gender of the baby and identify many abnormalities in the early months of pregnancy. Still, technology without clinical expertise is useless. British midwives are trained to practise also in areas where technology is the exception rather than the rule. Technology is a complement to midwifery practice rather than a substitute.

Joy and happiness are usually hallmarks of midwifery. Yet the practice is not exempt from woe, sorrow and disappointment. Some moments are bittersweet and fleeting, but none are forgotten by the parents and others who were part of those particular events. In Britain, morbidity and mortality in the mother and baby is not as common as it is in some other countries, but there is always the potential for a bad outcome to rear its ugly head at any stage of the childbearing process. I have had numerous exciting and rewarding experiences in midwifery, as well as some truly heartbreaking moments.

I can recall one situation that has left an indelible mark on my mind. It involved a beautiful baby boy. I will refer to him as Dave. Dave was born following an uncomplicated pregnancy, labour and delivery. He was placed in his mother's arms as soon as possible after birth to establish the initial contact of baby with mother. There is evidence to suggest that initial contact of a baby with the parents, especially the mother, is a critical element to the promotion of the bonding process. A bond needs to be initiated as soon as possible after birth because the bond dictates how the mother will care for her baby after birth and beyond. Fathers bond with their babies also, but the mother–infant bond is stronger and more acute for the baby's survival. Dave's parents were happy and doted on him as most parents do when a new baby arrives.

There was no evidence in his parents' history to indicate that there would be any problems with Dave. It is part of the established practice that a midwife performs a thorough examination of a new-born baby in addition to a complete post-delivery assessment of the baby's mother. The aim of the examination is to establish normality, to set baselines for the postnatal care of both mother and baby, to document the details for continuity of care, and to refer any potential problems to the doctor for further assessment and referral as and when appropriate.

I duly examined Dave, starting with his head and finishing at his toes. The examination of a baby's head includes checking the head measurements, eyes, mouth and other structures. When I examined

Dave's eyes, I was mesmerised by his long eyelashes – but, alas, there were no eyes in the sockets. Midwives are trained to disguise the presence of abnormalities until preparations are in place for the news to be communicated in an honest, uncomplicated, sensitive and gentle manner to the parents. I explained to Dave's parents that the doctor would need to re-examine Dave's head as I was concerned about his eyes. Following confirmation by the doctor that there were no eyes in Dave's eye sockets, the doctor first emphasised that there was normality in other structures apart from his eyes. The doctor then told the parents that Dave's eyes were absent. Congenital absence of the eyes, or anophthalmia, is a rare condition. An ophthalmologist or eye specialist must be the lead person in the confirmation of the diagnosis and formulation of the plan of action.

It is important to allow the parents to have time alone with the baby following the disclosure of bad news. This type of news is like a bereavement, a loss of the perfect baby. The doctor and I withdrew from the delivery room to afford Dave's parents some time alone. I was within close proximity, however, in case they required any assistance from me.

Some time later, the doctor and I returned to the delivery room. The doctor explained the process that would be involved with Dave's further assessment and progress. A coordinated effort between the midwife, the eye specialist, the health visitor and the paediatric specialist was required initially. As Dave developed, other support agencies would be involved with his care and progress. I delivered other babies who presented with other abnormalities in a small number of exceptional circumstances, but I did not encounter the condition of anophthalmia again. I always remember Dave and his long eyelashes.

By 1972, I was registered both as a nurse with the General Nursing Council and as a midwife with the Central Midwives Board in England, and had gained post-qualification experience mainly in nursing and some limited experience in midwifery practice. At this point I felt compelled to return to Barbados to use my skills to care for Bajans. I reasoned that the Barbados government was instrumental in my travelling to England and that I should repay the government and the people by offering to serve in the Barbados health service establishments. I returned to Barbados near the end of 1972, determined to enjoy the Christmas holiday in a typical Bajan manner with my family and friends. It was the first Christmas that I would spend in Barbados after six years of toil and struggle.

Working in Barbados in the 1970s

A few weeks after arriving in Barbados, I applied to the Barbados Nursing Council for registration to practise as a nurse and midwife and enquired about vacancies for registered nurses on the island. I joined the waiting list for a position at the Queen Elizabeth Hospital in Bridgetown and worked meanwhile as an occasional nurse in a country clinic and a satellite maternity clinic. Eventually I obtained a post in the intensive care unit of the main general hospital and worked there for about a year.

Working in the intensive care unit was a rewarding experience in terms of developing clinical expertise in caring for critically ill patients with conditions like tetanus, typhoid, kidney failure and heart failure. The patients ranged from newborn babies to the very elderly and the main reason for their presence in the intensive care unit was that their conditions were life-threatening. Most of the nurses and doctors in the unit were either natives who had returned from working in countries like the UK, USA or Canada, or expatriates and others who had a special interest in working in Barbados. The outstanding feature of the work was the close supporting relationship that existed between the doctors, nurses and support services. The main goal was to explore all avenues to bring about the speedy recovery of all the patients who arrived in the unit.

Unfortunately, we lost some of the patients in spite of the high quality of care. One loss that has always remained in my thoughts is a little baby boy who was ten days old and very critical with tetanus. I will refer to him as Lee. Lee had been delivered in the maternity unit and it was a mystery how he could have contracted tetanus. His parents could not identify any reason why he had contracted the illness, because they had cared for him at home in the same manner as they had cared for their other children.

Controlling and preventing muscle spasms is one of the main areas of care for patients with tetanus. The tetanus bacillus causes spasms of the body muscles, starting with the jaw muscles, hence the name 'lockjaw'. The critical effect is that the breathing muscles are also affected. This is very dangerous for all patients, but especially for a newborn baby who could easily suffer brain injury from lack of oxygen. Lee was everybody's baby in the unit, and the nurses and doctors toiled so hard to sustain him. Very sadly, Lee gave up the fight for life and we were all devastated for many days afterwards. It was a tragedy for his parents. Lee would have been more than thirty years old now if he had survived, and I still remember him with his little body contorted with the spasms as we battled to relax his muscles in an effort to save his life.

Tetanus is still a potential killer worldwide, and it is important for individuals to be immunised against the infection or given the tetanus antitoxin or antiserum when they sustain injuries that put them at risk of contamination of the site of the injury. A record of the date of administration of any tetanus injection is important for medical reasons. This is why the doctor always enquires about the date of the last tetanus injection when treating patients with injuries that breach the protective function of the skin. It is unquestionably better to prevent tetanus than to treat it, because it causes anguish in the patients and demands hard toil, diligence and dedication from all those who are involved in caring for them. Although the outcome of such hard toil was mainly positive, occasionally we were faced with negative outcomes like baby Lee's demise.

The work was indeed rewarding, but the costs to the carers were unquantifiable. Stress was one of those costs and in order to ensure equitable periods of respite for carers, everyone was exposed to similar hours of work. The working pattern in the intensive care unit in Barbados involved all nurses in the twenty-four-hour day. Barbados is a tropical island where the sun rises in the morning, shines all day and sets in the evening all year round apart from when it rains. It could therefore be very difficult for night-shift workers to sleep during the day. The working rota included a period of two weeks on the morning shift and one week on the afternoon shift followed by one week on the night shift. The cycle was then repeated and continued in this fashion all year round. There were three teams that covered the unit and a senior nurse headed each team. The team of doctors included specialists from medicine, surgery, anaesthetics, haematology, pathology and supporting specialists like physiotherapists and occupational therapists, with back-up services from hospitality and maintenance. The collaborative effort resulted in the recovery and discharge from the unit of a number of grateful patients. I remember this aspect of the work with pride as I made my contribution to the survival of several critically ill persons in Barbados. I wished that baby Lee was one of them.

I worked in Barbados for about two years, and although I enjoyed every moment of my experience of caring for patients there, I then decided to return to England for a brief period. After that I was planning to work in the USA, in order to broaden my experience of caring for a diverse patient population. Circumstances beyond my control, however, appeared to be shaping my future career path.

Teaching Nursing and Midwifery

I returned to London in the spring of 1974. I had formulated what I perceived to be the perfect plan: I would spend a few months in London before going to Florida in the USA to work as a registered nurse. While I was working in Barbados, I met some nurse colleagues who had worked in Florida – some were American, while others came from a variety of other countries including Jamaica, Trinidad and Tobago and the UK. We planned to have a reunion in Florida, but no plan is ever 'perfect', and ours was no exception. I never made the relocation to Florida. Instead I spent the next twenty-eight years in London, working as a nurse, a midwife, a teacher and finally a lecturer in a London university.

During my childhood, I had the firm belief that my real calling was to be a teacher. On several occasions when I attended church on Sunday, I helped the Sunday school teacher, Sister Hazel, with the activities and was invariably impressed by her approach to teaching the biblical lessons to the class. Sister Hazel was a slim, elegant young woman of about twenty-something years. She was always smiling and exuded a level of patience that I had never seen in any other adult at that time, so that even when she was unhappy with the behaviour of some of the diminutive rascals she found it difficult to form even a hint of an angry expression when she scolded them. She was a good role model and I believe that the early influence Sister Hazel exerted on my young life was a nurturing influence for my becoming a teacher and lecturer. A few years after I left Barbados, my mother wrote to me to say that Sister Hazel had married and had left our church.

Teaching nursing and midwifery is a peculiar but specific skill, because, like many other health disciplines, the theory and the practice bases can never be separated. To be a teacher of nursing or midwifery, a registered practitioner requires a combination of advanced knowledge and practice bases. When I trained to be a teacher in the early 1980s, the entry requirements to teacher training included significant clinical experience and the possession of an advanced diploma in the theory of nursing or midwifery, depending on the area of choice. By the time I left teaching, the requirements had been elevated to advanced clinical and theoretical knowledge in nursing or midwifery in addition to the possession of higher academic qualifications up to doctorate level. As part of my personal professional development during the period from the early 1980s until I left the profession, I had no option but to engage in the pursuit of academic excellence up to the level of MA (Master of Arts).

My career in teaching and lecturing started in the early 1980s with my selection by the head of the midwifery training school to work as a clinical teacher because I possessed the necessary qualifications. My work involved supporting students of nursing and midwifery in the clinical/ward environment on rotation to the day and night duty rotas. My remit was to assist students in a coherent way to relate their theoretical knowledge to the practice of the profession. I enjoyed the job immensely and realised that I needed to extend my development to become a registered teacher. I had obtained the necessary advanced theoretical diplomas both in nursing and midwifery, and in 1984 I entered university to undertake a one-year full-time course to become a qualified teacher. I was fortunate at that time because the government had a special fund designed to support student teachers from the nursing, midwifery and related professions like health visiting and community nursing, amongst others. The fund catered for the expenses of the course as well as the income of the student for the entire academic year. I graduated from the university in 1985 and began a qualified teaching career that lasted for more than twenty-three years.

During those years, the education and training of nurses and midwives was under constant change. The approach to education and training compared with that of the 1960s metamorphosed into a hybrid approach that was assimilated by institutions of higher education. The process was gradual, detailed and intense, starting with the government reorganisation of the NHS (National Health Service) which eventually cascaded down to education in the health professions. The central argument was that health care professionals should be fit for practice in the years beyond 2000 and this implied that the education should produce competent, effective practitioners. It was reasoned that the most appropriate setting would be an institution of higher education.

There was intense activity prior to the transfer to the higher education institutions. Schools of nursing and midwifery were amalgamated to form colleges. In the intervening period before assimilation into higher education, there was intense activity in the form of seminars, workshops, exchange visits to other colleges of nursing and midwifery and visits to universities to create awareness in teachers and other relevant personnel of the pending changes and the potential effects on the teachers, the students and most of all the delivery of client care. As with any change, there were anxieties about issues like salaries, conditions of service and pensions, and many people voiced their dissatisfaction with the proposed changes. The professional bodies, the professional unions and human resources personnel, amongst others, were involved in the change process. It was long, exhausting and sometimes bewildering, but the seminars and workshops continued. In spite of all the protests and anxieties, the colleges of nursing and midwifery were assimilated by the universities into appropriate faculties by the mid-1990s.

I observed that the significant difference in educating students of nursing and midwifery in a university setting was the management and approach to the process of learning. The main manager of the university was the vice chancellor, whereas the main manager of nursing and midwifery education prior to the assimilation was the chief executive. The university, however, was not functioning in isolation, because the regulatory bodies of nursing and midwifery education provided specific rules that governed education and training. The university had to operate within those parameters. The other significant changes that I observed were that teachers of nursing and midwifery were given the title of 'lecturer' and essentially had to be graduates. Many of them had secured graduate status during the years leading up to the transition, but those who were still non-graduates at the time of the assimilation were assisted by the university to secure graduate status. However, as the years progressed after the assimilation, graduate lecturers were encouraged to embark on other scholastic activities and these included qualifications up to doctorate level. Graduate status as a minimum was non-negotiable, however, because there were significant changes in the provision of educational courses in nursing and midwifery at diploma as well as at undergraduate level. Previously, courses were designed for certificate and diploma qualifications.

Teaching nursing and midwifery was a very rewarding experience for me. One comment that was bantered amongst some of my colleagues was that we should teach the students to the highest standard because they might be the nurses and midwives who delivered us, our children or grandchildren, or cared for us in the medical ward or the nursing care home when we became older.

One of the concepts of teaching that I learned during my teacher training was that learning was a relatively permanent change in behaviour which was a result of experience. Students come with a variety of personal skills, experiences, behaviours and motivations to learning opportunities. I observed over the years that these variables were usually modified by the end of a three-year nursing course or an eighteen-month post-registration midwifery course. Student feedback to lecturers is an essential element of monitoring the effectiveness of learning and teaching experiences. Invariably most students comment that they are very different individuals at the end of an educational experience as compared with the individuals they were at the start. Students of nursing and midwifery are no exception.

I always felt a sense of pride and achievement when a cohort of nurses or midwives graduated. It was especially rewarding to see them in their academic robes walking across the platform to receive their diplomas and degrees, and even more rewarding to observe them as they practised as registered nurses or midwives. Many of those same graduates progressed in the professions to become managers and lecturers and in so doing perpetuated the continuing progress in the health professions.

As a result of the immense change in the education and training of health care professionals and the provision of care for clients in the new millennium, I felt nostalgic about how far the professions had come since I started on my nursing journey in 1966. I became increasingly restless about revisiting the roots of my nursing career, and over several months I planned to make a return visit to Wakefield, Yorkshire.

The Visit

I arrived at London King's Cross station about half an hour before the scheduled train departure time. This was a good move, because I had to acclimatise to the surroundings and confirm the location of the platform. I had forgotten that the King's Cross I remembered from the 1960s and 70s was many light years away from the modern station! I was quietly impressed by the view of what is now King's Cross St Pancras International station as I made my way to the part of the station I needed, which is located on the other side of the street.

I boarded the British Rail East Coast electric express train to Wakefield Westgate at 09.35 hours on a summer's day in August. The day was greyish at first, but I did not really care about the weather because I was extremely excited about seeing Wakefield again. This would be the first time I had visited the city in more than forty years.

The visit was different in so many ways: I was considerably older, I was accompanied by my husband, and the train was an express travelling at about one hundred miles per hour in a peak summer month. The preparation for departure from King's Cross station was not unlike the preparation for take-off by a plane. The gates to the platform were closed a few minutes before the train departed, the seats in the train were numbered like those in an aircraft, and the team leader of the 09.35 trip recited safety information over the intercom.

I was prepared to log as many details of the journey as possible, and had ensured that I included enough writing materials in my luggage. As soon as the train departed from the platform my eyes feasted on every detail. I felt like a child in a toy shop. I noticed allotments, industrial and retail parks, playing fields, sewage works, waterways, factories, level crossings, gymkhana courses, car parks, electricity substations, mini lakes, anglers, forests, office complexes, graffiti, freightliners and houses without smoking chimneys. During my first journey to Wakefield in 1966, smoking chimneys had played a prominent part in what I had observed. Today it is relatively unusual to see a house with a smoking chimney.

I was acutely aware of the constant change in the accents and vernacular of people as passengers boarded or disembarked from the train during the journey. As the train got closer to Wakefield, I became even more aware of the familiar northern accent, easily recognisable to me even after all those years. The journey lasted a little over two hours, travelling through Stevenage, Peterborough, Grantham and Doncaster before arriving at Wakefield Westgate train station.

I felt an overwhelming flood of nostalgia as I stepped onto the platform. My husband was visiting

Wakefield for the first time and was interested only in seeing the city. The surroundings were different, though. The station looked modern and the activity was like that in any modern city train station. The staff members were as polite and helpful as I remembered and a kind middle-aged man gave clear instructions on how to get around the city.

It was refreshing to see that the city of Wakefield is now cleaner, more vibrant, developed and bustling. There is a free city bus, the Wakefield Metro, which makes it easy and economical to get around the main areas. Some areas in the city run on very steep gradients and I found that a greater measure of stamina was needed to cope with those areas now as compared with my ability to cope in those early years! My husband was no exception. He laboured as much as I did as we walked around those steep areas.

The first task during the trip was to revisit the site of the old hospital where I had my first nursing experiences. I already knew that the hospital had been demolished in the 1980s and the site had been sold on to property developers. The continued organisation and reorganisation in the NHS that started in the 1970s resulted in the closure of many establishments including some hospitals, especially small ones.

My husband and I took the number 102 Lubset bus to the site. I became emotional as soon as I saw the hospital site and felt bereft and angry that the hospital was no longer there. The site is now a housing estate with several streets lined with modern houses. The high iron gates that were there in the 1960s were still there, but formed part of a great enclosure for the housing estate. The high red-brick wall enclosed the estate just as it did previously for the hospital. A local man told us that during the property development the builders were instructed to retain the iron gates as a sort of historical monument. We spent some time walking around the estate, and the road that led from the main road to the estate appeared to be similar to the long path that I took to the hospital all those years ago.

When I felt I had seen enough, we caught another bus back to the city centre. The new Wakefield Market Hall was our next stop. The Market Hall is situated on Union Street and has an unusual structure that is predominantly metal. It is not beautiful and has a façade that screams 'utilitarian'. On the positive side, however, it is spacious and clean and offers easy pedestrian access. The market was not bustling as might be expected, but it may have been due to the recent opening of the facility. Perhaps in time the Market Hall will be full to capacity.

An important part of any visit is to locate a suitable place for refreshments. There were several places that would suit any palate, but we opted for one of the local fast-food restaurants. The food was hot, well cooked and satisfying. It replenished our dwindling energy stores.

We completed the trip with a visit to the Wakefield Northgate Cathedral, where we were given a brief tour by one of the volunteers from the cathedral shop. During the tour we paused to look at the sculpture of the Madonna and Child. After a period of quiet reflection and prayer, we purchased some souvenirs from the shop and then toured the courtyard, where memorial stones date back many centuries.

The evening was fast approaching when we decided to make our way to the Wakefield Westgate station for the return journey to London. As we wearily boarded the train, I mused on the significance of the visit. I felt that I had achieved my objective in that I had seen the old hospital site and had toured the city of Wakefield. I was impressed by the obvious development of the city, so different now from how I remembered it. I felt that I had somehow purged myself of any negative feelings remaining from my early experiences in Wakefield. I had come so far since then, and was glad to appreciate this more positive and mature attitude to my memories of the place.

The visit to Wakefield danced in my mind for many weeks and I remained emotionally charged. I was searching for reasons to explain my reactions to seeing Wakefield for the first time after so many years, and decided that I needed to test my feelings for Yorkshire against my feelings for one of the other cities which had been important to me during my early years in England. I chose to focus on Nottingham and the hospital where I continued nurse training when I left Yorkshire. After all, I had spent a longer period of time there than I had in Yorkshire.

Some time later, on a sunny but chilly morning, I returned with my husband to King's Cross and boarded another train heading north. The weather was typically ambivalent, but I was determined to remain positive about the trip in spite of the chill that was seeping into my bones. The high-speed passenger train eased its way out of the station and gathered speed. The route was similar to the one we had taken to Wakefield, but we had to change trains at Grantham for the Nottingham line. The scenery was familiar, but on this occasion I was preoccupied with the fields as the train raced along. I noticed some fields that were dark green, some that were brownish, and the startling contrast of the fluorescent yellow fields that were carpeted by blooming rapeseed plants. The yellow was accentuated by intermittent bursts of sunshine. I was fascinated by the colour of the rapeseed, which reminded me of a dress that I loved to wear as a child – made of soft pink material offset by yellow flounces. The dress has long gone, of course, but I still remember it as my favourite ever dress.

As the train continued to eat up the track, I caught glimpses of animals lazing or grazing in the fields. Heifers with their tiny calves nestling next to them; other heifers with prominent udders standing at ease; horses trotting in the fields, some kitted out in protective coats in a variety of colours. I realised that I was smiling: it seemed incongruous that horses would be kitted out in such an array of bright colours – colours that were more suited to a carnival procession.

The journey between London and Grantham lasted a little over an hour and the connecting train for

Nottingham was about thirty minutes away. While we were awaiting the arrival of the connecting train, my husband and I busied ourselves with beverages in the departure lounge at the station. We were so preoccupied with our discussion about Nottingham that we did not realise that the Nottingham train had in fact arrived at a platform lower down the station than we had anticipated. When a station police officer confirmed where the train was berthed, we ran like demented beasts. We were unaware that the train guard had been watching our lightning sprint, and when he checked our tickets he gleefully repeated the sequence of events, from our speaking to the police officer to our mad scramble to board the train. We were so dumbfounded by his accurate tale of the two frantic passengers that we collapsed in fits of laughter to hide our embarrassment. The guard appeared to be relishing the fact that he had convinced us we had provided the whole world with a spectacular performance, while we continued with our bursts of laughter. We were still laughing when the train pulled out of the station, and the memory still makes me smile.

It was a slow rural train and stopped at some stations that appeared very remote compared to the busyness of some of the other stations we had passed. Again there were fields, some with the ever-present fluorescent yellow of rapeseed plants. The journey ended as quickly as it had begun and as the train approached its last stop, Nottingham, I found myself devoid of any emotion as I prepared to disembark. I decided to leave things to unfold naturally.

The walk from the platform to the exit was a mean trek and when I emerged from the station I felt as though I was visiting the city for the first time. The only landmark that I recognised was the red-brick wall that separated the station exit from the main road. Many years previously, I had taken a black taxi from the same location to the hospital where I continued nurse training after leaving Wakefield. The black taxis were still visible, but my husband and I opted for the local bus. I was anxious to reach the hospital in order to test my theory about my emotional reaction to Nottingham. How different would it be from Wakefield?

The town centre was extremely clean and ordered. The central bus station was a bustle of people and buses arriving and departing from the several platforms that dotted the spacious site. There were also cars going in and out of the multi-storey car park which formed part of the station complex. I noticed a group of bus drivers who were engrossed in deep chatter, but my husband and I decided to ask them for directions to the appropriate bus in order to save time. They gave us precise instructions as they took turns to describe different phases of the journey. One bus driver appeared to be the comedian in the group and playfully suggested that we should ride on his bus because he was the best driver in that 'chattering' group. We discovered that there was a free bus service between the two main hospitals in Nottingham and relished the free bus ride. I was impressed by the patience and lack of urgency in the way that both passengers and bus drivers conducted themselves; in that respect, things had not changed very much from when I lived in Nottingham decades before.

When the bus drew near the hospital I recognised some of the landmarks, but I was surprised at the 'newness' of the surroundings. I was preoccupied with trying to match what I saw with the images that I had stored in the recesses of my memory, but it was like a difficult jigsaw puzzle and I was experiencing difficulty fitting some of the pieces into place. I recognised the path that led to the hospital at first, but as the free bus made its way down the hospital drive I became confused and disappointed because I could see radical changes in the surroundings. There were now several hospital streets, a variety of complexes of specialist units, a large car park with barriers and payment machines, and a new maternity unit that formed part of one of the main complexes. I had taken some photographs from the 1970s with me, to act as pointers to some of the locations as I remembered them, but the photographs were unhelpful because the changes in the surroundings were so extensive.

I was disappointed because things were different from what I had anticipated, but on the other hand I was happy that the hospital in Nottingham still existed, even though it was a modern version of what I recalled. It occurred to me that I could compare the surroundings in the hospital complex with that of a human going through the stages of life from childhood to old age, but the process was in the reverse for the Nottingham hospital because, instead

117

of ageing, it had reverted to its infancy, a new beginning. By comparison, the hospital in Wakefield had not survived and perhaps that was one of the reasons why I had experienced such acute emotions when I visited that site. I had lived in Nottingham far longer than I had lived in Yorkshire and had explored Nottingham – especially with my friend Winnie – far more than I had explored Yorkshire, and yet I did not experience the type of intense emotional reaction that I had when I visited Wakefield.

As I thought further about this, I theorised that Wakefield was the place where I was socialised into the British/English culture and nursing. 'Socialisation' as a concept in this context is appropriate, I feel. It is a process by which an individual acquires the culture of the surrounding society, and although the process is a lifelong one, the early years in an individual's life are the most significant. During the early years, the basic foundations are laid and those foundations have a profound influence on the entire socialisation process. I concluded that my early years in Wakefield (my teenage/young adult years) were the critical years of my socialisation into the British/English culture and therefore my feelings towards Wakefield would be more enduring and intense than my feelings for other cities in Britain/England. I did not feel that I needed to purge myself of any negative feelings about Nottingham because I had already completed that purging process when I visited Wakefield. I had balanced the theorem, *quod erat demonstrandum*, and I had reached the haven of complete peace.

When we had completed our visit to the hospital, my husband and I boarded the free bus back to the city centre and began to search for refreshment. We opted for the fish and chips restaurant that was near the station and ordered two big slabs of fish and two portions of chips. By then we were considerably famished. I was so preoccupied with savouring the food with its typical northern taste that I was oblivious of my husband and the other customers in the restaurant. It did not matter that the fish portion was small compared to the coating of batter that had enveloped it; I enjoyed every mouthful, just as I had done when we student nurses had eaten fish and chips from newspaper parcels and then crawled sluggishly to the train station.

The return train journey was quicker than the outward trip because the train was a direct route to London with fewer stops. I reflected quietly about my visit. By the time the train pulled in to King's Cross station, I felt that the journey had been worth the effort. My husband and I walked through the bustling throng of passengers and out of the station. The evening was noticeably chilly but pleasant as we made our way to the underground station for the final leg of our journey home.

Reflections

I tend to describe my experiences as being in the good-bad old days. Compared with the situation that exists in the caring professions in the new millennium, those earlier days were by comparison more clearly defined. I am not proclaiming on the rooftop that they were the best days, but certainly they were tolerable to me – perhaps because I had nothing with which to compare them.

Today there are several factors that have significantly influenced the ethos of nursing and midwifery education and care provision. These factors include:

the use of technology;
the increase in bureaucracy;
the change in the management structure;
the extending role of the nurse and midwife;
the change in family structure;
a more critically aware patient/client population;
changes in working patterns;
greater ethnic diversity in clients and carers;
increasingly higher expectations of the care providers by the clients/patients, their relatives and friends.

Many of the nurses and midwives of my era have retired and unfortunately this phenomenon, together with scarce resources and specialised care, has led to an acute shortage of experts in both nursing and midwifery. Persistent shortage and its consequences are frequently highlighted in the media through debate by patients, their relatives, professionals and voluntary organisations.

There are two factors that appear to be most significant in the perceived shortage of nurses and midwives, namely the use of technology and the extending role of the nurse and midwife. Technology is now an integral part of care provision, hence carers have to employ the technology in caring for patients/clients as well as documenting the care that was delivered to their assigned patients/clients. There has been debate about the use of technology at the expense of the amount of time spent on personal involvement, and claims that technology has overtaken the application of sound clinical judgement to practice. Some argue that technology has become an integral part of care provision yet should not be used as a substitute for clinical judgement, but rather as a complement to clinical practice.

The extending role of the nurse and midwife implies that many tasks that were originally performed by doctors are now being performed by nurses and midwives. Some examples of this extending role include nurses prescribing medication and midwives repairing lacerations associated with childbirth, as well as performing medical examinations of newborn babies. The extending role is not

122

without consequences. There is now increased professional accountability and responsibility as well as higher patient expectations, resulting in an increase in litigious situations involving nurses and midwives.

Another significant change in the professions is the approach to racism and racist behaviour. Although there was evidence of overt racism during my early experience, as I discussed earlier in the book, there was still a general respect for nurses, regardless of their colour, creed or gender. I reasoned that then, patients and their families were more dependent on the carers and were not as informed as patients and their families are now.

There is today a marked difference in the concept of racism as compared with the good-bad old days. This is not to argue that racism has been eradicated, but rather to suggest that racism is no longer tolerated as it might have been during my early years in the nursing profession. There are transparent legal measures in place to neutralise racist behaviour, but the obverse of this is that there is apparent paranoia and mistrust in some organisations – with the unfortunate result that individuals are at risk of becoming scapegoats in order to appease complainants if there is any allegation of wrongdoing in the organisation.

The carers have a duty to inform patients of all aspects of their care so that they can make informed choices about the advice and care available to them. Care is designed to be client-driven rather than carer-driven, but it is debatable that care may be driven by available resources and organisational constraints.

The media and other such technologies have eroded the secrecy that previously existed in health care settings. There are established procedures where patients can demand to see their care records. There are consequences of this for nurses, midwives and other carers. They have to ensure that they always protect themselves and the clients through precise, truthful and contemporaneous documentation of all aspects of care that they provide; that they maintain their professional integrity and competence; that they seek professional assistance when they are unsure of any aspects of their practice; that they treat all individuals with respect and dignity.

The current approach to ridding the caring professions of unsuitable workers is to perform a CRB (Criminal Records Bureau) investigation on all prospective workers who are in contact with the public. Nurses and midwives are included in this type of pre-employment screening and although this tool has been effective in safeguarding the public, occasionally a miscreant outwits the system with undesirable consequences to others. Fortunately situations like this are rare.

The old public opinion was that the typical nurse was in the business because she cared like Florence Nightingale did. As a result of that opinion, many people said that nurses were 'worth their salt' and were underpaid. It was not unusual for nurses to visit the butcher's shop and be given pig's trotters and other such extras free of charge. The shop proprietors and market stallholders had an uncanny knack of identifying 'the nurse'. Certainly, in my case and in those times, it was not difficult to identify my trade, as I was black. It was the general opinion in Wakefield in the 1960s that young black females were usually nurses. I did not mind, however, because I was always game for a freebie!

Currently, the public generally believe that nurses are well paid compared with other care workers. No longer can nurses expect concessions like those I enjoyed in the 1960s, 70s or even 80s. Nurses are expected to pay as much as, or even more, than the general public.

Changes occurred in the provision of nursing education in the 1970s to cater for a more diverse population in the years beyond 2000. The education was designed to teach carers to recognise racist behaviour and act appropriately to avoid creating scenarios that might be perceived as racist. Unfortunately, there are still occasions when evidence of prejudice rears its head, with dire consequences for those who are affected, be they the victim or the perpetrator of the behaviour.

There were no security guards in the hospital environment in those days. The ward orderlies dealt with any form of violence, and violence was the exception rather than the rule. Police presence then was only evident in the Casualty department when patients who were victims of violence were brought in for treatment, or when patients or visitors became a danger to the hospital personnel.

Nurses and midwives are now at risk of overt abuse, and that abuse may be verbal, emotional or even physical. The abuse, however, is not exclusive to nurses. Other health care professionals are as much at risk as they are. It is arguable that, given the evidence to suggest that the world is now a more violent place, as long as people exist there is the potential for violent behaviour in some individuals, and that nurses and midwives should expect to be at risk as much as the general public because they deal with a variety of people in a variety of situations. Others argue that violence in society must not and cannot be tolerated in any circumstance because there are consequences to the victim, the perpetrator and significant others.

There is debate about whether or not financial remuneration increases job satisfaction. Nurses and midwives are better rewarded for the work that they do today, although the level of pay is relative to the economic climate of the twenty-first century. There is anecdotal evidence that many nurses and midwives are dissatisfied with the environment that exists in hospitals, in spite of the reasonable returns that they receive. In recent times, the position of the matron has been reinvented. The rationale for the matron was that she would create an environment that would enhance care provision and boost staff morale. There is evidence to suggest, however, that the outcome has not been as fruitful as was anticipated when the idea for reintroduction was first conceived. Some media reports still highlight patient and staff dissatisfaction with care and care provision.

When I reflect on the events that occurred during my working life in Britain, I see my success as a release from the shackles of the past rather than as a triumph. My successes have reinforced the belief that I had during those early learning years. The belief was that I could reach my goals in the nursing and midwifery professions if I endured – and yes, I made it, against all odds. You may ask me if I wish that things had been different. I would answer without hesitation that I do not regret any of my experiences because they have moulded me into the person I have become: a critically aware and very grateful individual.

I wanted to share some of my reflections, ideas and feelings about my years in England, especially the 1960s when love was in the air and young people were preoccupied with peace and love. Perhaps that preoccupation masked the reality of the life that existed in nursing in England; perhaps it desensitised us to the reality of the situation in order that we could survive in an 'alien' environment. Some readers may have experienced feelings like mine many years ago; some may be having those feelings today. Human nature is such that as long as diversity exists in race, creed, culture, colour, age and gender, humans will continue to discriminate. The more mature in spirit learn to live with diversity for the benefit of the individual and the world.

I always try to express my gratitude to God for my successes as well as my failures and disappointments. Life in the nursing and midwifery professions has been a great teacher in terms of spiritual, social, educational and personal development. Over the years I have learned to use my failures and dis-appointments as stepping stones to greater things, and to use my successes to help others whenever I perceive that they are experiencing situations similar to those that I have encountered over the last forty years.

I have realised that even when others are experiencing situations that are similar to those that I encountered, they are operating in an environment that is totally different from the one to which I was exposed – yet untainted principles like self-management, self-respect, tolerance, patience, impartiality and humility still hold firm. Qualities like these were the sustaining factors in my life and development during those years.

I visited Barbados recently for a family occasion. I was very excited to renew my contact with some of the original Wakefield party group, including Bentfield. I discovered that some of the group are now retired, some are on the edge of retirement, and others are continuing in the business of nursing and midwifery as senior managers, chief executives, senior lecturers and professors. Some have broken away completely from the business of nursing and midwifery and have no regrets about the changes. Some of the people in the group are now entrepreneurs and entertainers. We are planning to have a big party for the Wakefield group in the near future. We see ourselves as pioneers of multicultural nursing in Yorkshire. We are the successful survivors.

Today I sit on the edge of retirement. I reflect on those days when my future in nursing in England was somewhere out there in a fathomless abyss. The blackness of that abyss was impenetrable and I could not contemplate the eventual outcome of the many years of toil, sweat and tears. I believe passionately that the first West Indian immigrants, who arrived on the SS *Empire Windrush* or later in the middle of the twentieth century, paved the way for people like me to make a success of the opportunity to live and work in England, Great Britain, the United Kingdom, the 'mother country'. I feel that I was able to maintain the tradition of West Indian survival in a host country. I will always believe that I survived and succeeded because I was a granddaughter of the SS *Empire Windrush*.